A 2020 VISION IN A CHRISTIAN *Marriage*

A Past, Present, and Future Perspective

DR. HENRY L. AND
SUSAN M. TOWNSEND

WESTBOW
PRESS®
A DIVISION OF THOMAS NELSON
& ZONDERVAN

WestBow Press books may be ordered through booksellers or by contacting:

WestBow Press
A Division of Thomas Nelson & Zondervan
1663 Liberty Drive
Bloomington, IN 47403
www.westbowpress.com
844-714-3454

Scripture taken from the King James Version of the Bible.

Scripture quotations marked (NLT) are taken from the Holy Bible, New Living Translation, copyright ©1996, 2004, 2015 by Tyndale House Foundation. Used by permission of Tyndale House Publishers, a Division of Tyndale House Ministries, Carol Stream, Illinois 60188. All rights reserved.

Interior Image Credit: Cecelia Emery

ISBN: 978-1-6642-2899-3 (sc)
ISBN: 978-1-6642-2900-6 (hc)
ISBN: 978-1-6642-2898-6 (e)

Library of Congress Control Number: 2021906271

Print information available on the last page.

WestBow Press rev. date: 5/28/2021

And the Lord God said, "It is not good that the man should be alone;

I will make him and help meet for him."

—Genesis 2:18 (KJV)

CONTENTS

CONTENTS

INTRODUCTION

This marriage series is focused on a 2020 vision of the past, present, and future ramifications of marriage and family in Christian living. Faith is emphasized in order to help the readers gain a greater understanding of the precepts that lead to a stronger marriage. The principles used in this outline are applied to make it real as it relates to the husband and wife, siblings, parents and children, and how they all relate. The authors bring nearly fifty years of experience living and participating in an active role of Christian development in marriage.

There are many discussions, questions, and activities that may or may not be gender specific that relate to scripture. This series may lead to questions with contrasting viewpoints that will contribute to a broader, more insightful way of thinking of how we view ourselves as Christians in marriage. The entire series is written with the understanding that prayer in all topics and issues presented is all encompassing and is the first and last option to the success of all elements of marriage and family.

Chapter 1 Outline

God's Original Purpose in Marriage

A. Creation
   1. Man
   2. Woman
B. Garden of Eden
   1. Alignment with God
   2. Misalignment (The Fall)
   3. Marriage

References

Genesis 2:18; Matthew 19:5; Hebrews 13:4; Mark 10:7, 8; Ephesians 5:3; 1 Corinthians 7:1–40

Discussion

This chapter introduces a greater insight into God's reasons for placing a man in His earthly kingdom. God adds a woman to His design and invokes the presence of marriage for Adam and Eve, the first man and first woman on the planet. Then comes the first sin, which will be investigated from a marital point of view.

Objectives

Upon review of this chapter, the participants will achieve the following objectives:

1. Have a better understanding of God's original intention for marriage

2. Reflect on God's purpose for the creation of Adam and Eve in the garden of Eden
3. Compare Eden to marriage (the honeymoon)
4. Discuss living in alignment or misalignment in marriage

Questions

1. Is your marriage currently an Eden? If not, how can you make it so?
2. How was misalignment created in the garden of Eden?
3. List the misalignments that can be seen in marriages.
4. What makes your marriage more harmonious?
5. What takes away from the harmony?

CHAPTER 1

God's Original Purpose in Marriage

The book of Genesis draws a beautiful example of the first man and woman placed on earth by God. He created them as one in marriage. The setting is in the garden of Eden, where sin does not exist.

In the framework of a creation without sin, this paradise was created by God with the understanding that harmony with God must first be established among all who exist in His kingdom.

The correlation that exists with modern Christian marriages is that couples must first believe in God and Christ. Sharing a belief system enables couples to be of one accord and yoked together in Christ. The result of this union in marriage is manifested in the initial alignment with God, as it was with Adam and Eve (Gen. 2:18, 21–25).

In the Bethel Bible Study series, alignment or harmony is portrayed as fourfold in nature in the garden of Eden. First there must be harmony with God, then harmony with self, harmony with others, and harmony with nature. In order for a marriage to be in complete harmony, all the above must be in alignment. You must be obedient to God to have perfect harmony with Him; then you will have harmony with self. There is a sense of satisfaction in always being in the presence of God.

Harmony with others means being in harmony with your spouse—that is, the other person to whom you have given your life. If you understand that in marriage, spouses are as one, then one becomes self

(Gen. 2:23–24). Harmony with others also includes family members and other people in general.

Please note that in marriage, "self" is man and wife. You have individual qualities, likes and dislikes, but you compromise and maintain harmony as one.

Metaphorically speaking, in nature, harmony with God creates a serene and peaceful condition, illustrated by a beautiful lake scene or mountain view. This may be in the home, neighborhood, church, and community. The goal is to create a garden of Eden in your home and marriage, full of love from God.

This will be an ongoing process. It can come close to perfection only by placing God first in the marriage. It is important to reason that when you are in one accord with God, self, others, and nature, you will become as peaceful as Adam and Eve in the garden of Eden.

In the Bethel Bible Study series, insightful examples are constructed of how God's perfect place, the garden of Eden, may be changed to a place of enmity. This is a place associated with estrangement issues resulting from disharmony or misalignment with God, self (you and your spouse), others, and finally nature. Estrangement is in the culture and climate of the spheres we exist in (e.g., the home, the church, the place of worship, the work environment, and the community).

In a marriage, when disharmony creates estrangement issues with God, other factors may become out of alignment. Disharmony with self creates friction with self. Then disharmony with others becomes more apparent.

We also have disharmony with the environment or society as a whole (Gen. 3:15–18). We may have liberty to say it was sin that brought about disharmony with God and resulted in enmity with all.

Misalignment becomes an issue in your daily pursuit of happiness. We strongly suggest that you stay connected with God in Jesus Christ in everything you do. Keep the Lord in alignment and always go to Him first. When you do so, spiritual favor from above will enter your marriage with abundant blessings.

Chapter 2 Outline

Creation of Marriage by God

    A. Definition of Marriage
        1. Covenant versus Contract
    B. Purpose
        1. What God Wants for Us and What We Want for Our Marriage
        2. The Relationship
            a. Permanence
            b. Submission
    C. Reasons for Marriage
        1. Security
        2. Vindication (Getting Even)
        3. Love
        4. Companionship (A Helpmate)
        5. Mate Sent by God
        6. Money
        7. Physical Appearance
        8. "Shotgun Marriage"

References

Ephesians 5:21–33; Hebrews 13:4–7; Genesis 1:27–28, 2:18, 1 Peter 3:1–7; Proverbs 18:22; Mark 10:6–9; 1 Timothy 3:9–15

Discussion

This chapter discusses the meaning of marriage and the difference between covenant versus contract in holy matrimony. Reasons for God's design from the beginning will be compared to the cardinal reasons for humankind. The need to have a helpmate varies, and all may be considered in the framework of God's plan. In the book of Genesis, marriage is described as existing between the first people in the Bible, who are Adam and Eve, man and woman.

Objectives

Upon review of this chapter, the participants will achieve the following objectives:

1. Have a broader understanding of the meaning of marriage in a biblical sense
2. List components that make up a good marriage
3. Construct an atmosphere in marriage of spiritual growth and development
4. Explain the meaning of submission in marriage

Questions

1. What do you consider to be the major components of marriage in the sight of God?
2. What type of climate or atmosphere would you construct in an ideal marriage?
3. What are your views of submission in marriage?
4. What is your personal view of the meaning of marriage?

CHAPTER 2

Creation of Marriage by God

Marriage Defined

Marriage is a contract that pledges one to another in a binding agreement approved by both parties. Marriage is specifically designed by the Holy Bible to unite a man and a woman in a life of love and togetherness as long as they live. This is a commitment endured in life and sanctioned by God.

The word *contract* is defined by Merriam-Webster as a binding agreement that connects two or more people or parties together. The term and conditions are expressed in the contract. Legal agreements are conditional in case they are broken.

Marriage, according to the Bible, is the union of a man and a woman only. It is the nature of life's manifestation to yearn for companionship, a helpmeet, a person to live with and to plan a future with. Marriage is the act of sharing the most beautiful essence of God's creation together. The manifestation of a marriage of love extends itself into having someone who is always with you through the hardships of life and the successes that the Lord provides.

The union of holy matrimony is represented in the love that Christ has for the church. This love for each other is built on the grace that God gave us along with His Son, Jesus Christ. Marriage is not a perfect institution; however, it has the capacity to grow and develop with the partners in love and appreciation for each other. This appreciation is not codependence, but an expression of the love of God in your marriage—in everything you do as a couple.

Marriage in Christ is not primarily a legal, binding, social contract.

> Christians view marriage as a covenant made under God and in the presence of fellow members of the Christian family. It becomes a pledge taken by two Christian individuals that endures because the covenant is made unconditionally, pursuant to, and not be a force of the law, not in fear of actions from the marital agreement. The marriage covenant is more sacred, more binding, and more permanent than any legal contract that reflects the love of Christ. In other words, a covenant is made for life. We all know we will make mistakes and poor choices along the way, but in marriage you can have a sort of peace of mind that your unconditional love for each other will see you through it.(Wright and Roberts, 1997)

A biblically based marriage is one that is in balance with Christ as the head of the church. The biblical concept of marriage is oneness between two individuals that illustrates the oneness of Christ with His church: 1 + 1 = 1.

Reasons for Marriage

There are a variety of reasons why people get married. One may first think of love or even love at first sight. This is a good reason with biological undertones. Love at first sight occurs when you see that beautiful woman or handsome man. Appearance is the first sense appealing to your mind and consciousness. The beautiful person looks perfect and affects your hormones. Then your heart feels something as well. It's love! You have found that perfect person!

Or have you?

Other people decide to marry to make themselves feel secure. Security and monetary reasons for marriage are dated concepts. Those were most important during a time when men were the ones "bringing home the bacon" and women were encouraged to stay home and raise the children. Today, that isn't necessarily so. Women hold their own in the workforce on all levels. So, the notion of security may apply to both the male and the female in marriage.

Vindication, or getting back at a lost person with whom one has had a past affair, is a motivation for marriage that can be reckless and dangerous, especially when children come into the equation.

Companionship (a helpmate) may become a reason after all the games have been played and you are in an age bracket when most of your friends have children and appear to be in happy marriages. There is something comforting in knowing someone and having him or her by your side.

A "shotgun marriage" at one time was used when a couple discovered that a child had been conceived from an out-of-wedlock union before the man has asked for the woman's hand in marriage. The term is no longer used. Today there are many marriage ceremonies in which the bride is at the altar while pregnant, or even has a son as her ring bearer or a daughter as her flower girl. Nevertheless, let the marriage proceed.

Whatever may be the main reason for your marriage, we encourage you to take it to the Lord first. He will bless you with a good mate as He has blessed the authors of this book. Whatever you decide, make God your witness and hold true to your own.

Please avoid reasons that affect others. Case in point: I had two friends in college who were dating freely. They encountered two lovely young ladies. The two ladies were so close that one could not do anything without the other's OK. They made a pact that if one married one of the guys, the other lady would marry the other guy. They carried through in this pact. Then, during the course of the marriages, one lady said to the other, "If you have a baby, I will also have a baby." They did this too, without talking to their husbands. As the years went on, the marriages encountered difficult times and their relationships became dicey. At this point one lady said to the other, "If you get a divorce, I will also." So, they both did.

We encourage all young people who are considering marriage to be true to their mates and true to themselves and the Lord who created both partners. Let that be your reason for marriage.

Chapter 3 Outline

Understanding the Differences between Spouses in Marriage

    A. Marital Impact on the Culture and Climate
    B. Attitudinal Adjustments to Each Other
    C. Interpersonal Relations in Marriage
    D. Effect of Professional Careers on Marriage
        1. Respective Roles
        2. Role Reversal
        3. Keeping It Real
    E. Cultural Differences in Marriage
        1. Mixed Marriages
        2. Blended Marriages

References

Ephesians 4:2; 1 Corinthians 13:4–13

Discussion

This chapter deals with reconciliation in marriage and to some degree making concessions for each other. Attitude adjustments and interpersonal relationships come into play. The impact of professional careers and respective roles can have a negative or positive impact on marriage as God would have it.

Objectives

Upon review of this chapter, the participants will achieve the following objectives:

1. Understand that God's plan for marriage in a biblical sense still holds true
2. Develop a keen awareness of the negative and complicated impact of our culture on marriage
3. Become more keenly aware of the uniqueness of their spouses, learning their ways and how they act
4. Explain the meaning of "cleaving" to each other as we leave our parents
5. Explain how keeping Christ in marriage helps you to adjust to your partner's differences

Questions

1. Do we leave our parents and cleave to each other? What about the in-laws?
2. Would the presence of Jesus Christ in your marriage help you to adjust to your partner's differences?
3. What do you accept from your spouse in your marriage? If something is unacceptable, how do you incorporate a change?
4. Does ambition have a negative or positive impact on your arrangement in marriage?

CHAPTER 3

Understanding the Differences between Spouses in Marriage

People don't quite fit together like jigsaw puzzles. Personality is unique to each individual. You and your spouse bring your own differences to the marriage. Your individual uniqueness can be viewed by your spouse as "flaws in your character"—or, as a couple, you can view these differences as opportunities for growth.

The differences between us are determined by many external factors. These factors include family influences, cultural differences, work environment, personal preferences, and exposure. The way you grew up and the way your family handled various situations play a large role in how you individually will handle situations with your spouse. You may choose to follow your parents' example or choose another method.

Cultural influences tend to remain embedded in our lives and can play a large role in the way we go about choosing a mate and how we treat that mate. Culture can be defined in a couple of ways. One is ethnic background; another is the social climate we live in. These factors can determine whether you become a chauvinistic husband, a dominant wife, or a respectful partner. Both influence your makeup and may require adjustments in the marriage.

If Christ is at the center for both partners, you will be better able to adjust to your partner's differences. Having Christ in your marriage will help you develop better traits and habits, become more accepting of each other's differences, and show respect for each other in your differences. You learn to have forgiveness, patience, acceptance, tolerance, and willingness to compromise because you love each other.

In some cases, the career you choose will be driven by the educational opportunities you have and your exposure to things that are different from what your own experience has been. Your work environment may include people from all walks of life. They will impose their beliefs and opinions on you, and you must learn to discern what things you will keep as a part of you and what things you won't.

These things and more will determine who you will uniquely become and what you will bring to the marriage relationship. It is important that you include God in each choice that you make. When the time comes to consider marriage, many of these choices will have a bearing. One of the first things to consider is the families you each come from. Genesis 2:24 reminds us that a man shall "leave his father and his mother, and shall cleave unto his wife: and they shall be one flesh." The role of each spouse's parents must be determined and defined.

Marriage encourages the need to feel complete because of what the other person has to offer. Their differences can balance and complete you. What role did each of you expect of the other in marriage? Did this come from the way your parents were in their marriage? Is this different from the way your parents were? Was your choice of role in any way influenced by your career?

The differences and individualism of each spouse are somewhat developed through learned experience during the courtship period, through the honeymoon period, and into marital life itself.

During the courtship period, couples are driven by the five senses, accompanied by runaway hormones and the adjustment from adolescence to adulthood. Both the man and the woman put on their best behavior and their best appearance, offering compliments and thoughtfully extended courtesies. These things happen over a prolonged period of time.

When a couple gets married and takes a vow under God in holy matrimony, this covenant locks in all of the likes and dislikes—all of the good, the bad, and the ugly baggage that neither spouse knows the other has. This baggage slowly seeps out, and it creates harmonies and disharmonies throughout the marriage. Managing this newfound knowledge of your spouse may bring you closer to each other, or it may drive you apart. Your differences can cause conflict.

Differences of opinion and methods of solving problems will arise. How the spouses discuss, argue about, and resolve problems will determine the course of their marriage.

The uniqueness of marriage varies. Some may respond to simple adjustments. Examples could be preferring different kinds of food for dinner, or different styles of clothing to be worn in public, or different selections in television programming.

Acceptance in love, respect, and devotion is key in the development of a growing marital relationship. The ability to take all things to God in a loving relationship and identify, together, things you can live with and things you can't is crucial to a lasting marriage. It starts with what God will allow in your marriage. Couples must be cognizant of keeping a marriage pleasing to God and not necessarily to friends and relatives.

There is a misconception about the perfect marriage. It does not exist. Regardless of the coupling effect based on class and status, the fact of being yoked together—not as beasts of burden, but in a Christlike fashion—means a marriage is a work in progress. It requires real-time adjustment to your partner's idiosyncrasies or quirks, which may be offensive or disturbing from time to time.

In contemplating marriage, I hope you made a list or plan about your ideal partner years before you finally met them. Such plans should go far beyond the physical makeup of the perfect partner. Personality, interests, hobbies, and the social aspect of friends all come into play.

The uniqueness of your partner may provide an opening to a world that you never knew. But first, put God in your life. Pray together and worship together in church, and find couples who do the same. Try things that your spouse introduces you to in the form of travel, food, arts, entertainment, and sports. A good, healthy relationship depends on sharing each other's likes and dislikes and accepting some things about your partner that are not detrimental to your marriage. It is important to make concessions and try not to be one way or always have your way.

The ability to accept differences takes on even greater dimensions in a blended family. Acceptance is carried over to children from previous marriages. Both partners must accept, learn about, and understand the children and their personalities as they adjust to new members of the family. As you love your spouse and all that comes with him or her, you accept and love your spouse's children. It is important to keep God in the midst of the new family. Go the extra mile and support all of the kids, from Little League games to piano recitals. Be there for everyone with unconditional love. It doesn't come easy, but with God's help, keep on loving and praying together. Worship together and create a home environment with family harmony, free from external secular pressures. God smiles on young families that grow in the admonition of His grace. God watches over families, and He knows your heart.

Chapter 4 Outline

What Love Has to Do with It

- A. Philia
- B. Eros
- C. Storge
- D. Agape
- E. Manifestations of the types of Love
  1. Intimacy
  2. Songs of Solomon

References

Proverbs 5:18–19, 17:17; John 3:16; 1 Corinthians 13:1–12; Song of Solomon chapters 1–8, Romans 12:10

Discussion

This chapter identifies and discusses the four types of love, as exemplified in the Bible, and compares them to how we love our spouses. The greatest example of love is described in John 3:16, The illustration is set for us to follow. Intimacy and Songs of Solomon are used as metaphors to further illustrate the manifestations of the process.

Objectives

Upon review of this chapter, the participants will achieve the following objectives:

1. Define four types of love, as written in the Bible
2. Explain how these types of love are used interchangeably

3. Understand how one partner cannot exist without the other in marriage in the sight of God

Questions

1. What kind of love is exhibited in John 3:16?
2. What kind of love did Jesus exhibit in Luke 23:34?
3. Can you find other verses in the Bible that exemplify each type of love?

CHAPTER 4
What Love Has to Do with It

What's love got to do with it? *Love*!

Love has everything to do with it: "For God so loved the world that He gave his only begotten Son that whosoever believeth in Him would not perish, but have everlasting life" (John 3:16 KJV). You see, God loved us so much that He brought His Son down from heaven to personally share His love for all of us. Jesus talked to us and taught us how to love one another. Jesus then laid down His life for all of humanity, to save us from our sins and thus enable us to be with Him in the kingdom of heaven after death.

Love has everything to do with it, in the context of marriage between a man and a woman. It may be an emotional feeling initially, binding intangibles of the one you are attracted to. Can you recall when you really felt the initial urge to say the words "I love you" to the person you married? What meaning was attached to that word? How did you mean it? Were you just caught up in the moment?

I am sure in most cases your "I love you" came straight from your heart, full of all the emotions that got you to the point of expressing true feelings. This was a true phrase to use, not like the secret code used in the James Bond thriller *You Only Live Twice*. Yes, I love you.

Let us explore the various types of love as defined by mortals and then clarify them with divine discernment and righteous living in a Christian marriage.

Philia

Philia means close friendship or brotherly love in the Greek language according to Webster. Philia is one of the forms of love that is found throughout the New Testament. Christians are encouraged to love fellow Christians with brotherly affections—not to outdo one another but to show honor to one another.

Philia also means "friendship" or "affection." In the context of marriage, people who have fallen in love quite often have been friends first. We lack empirical data to prove it, but it happens. Friends who support each other through hard times and good times feel a certain closeness. Individuals who become psychological safety nets for one another after a bad relationship become closer. Some refer to this as codependency.

In regards to marriage, you have to like the person you marry, first. Sometimes after marriage, a friendship develops through raising children and other life experiences. The love you express to each other should be warm and show affection, like brothers and sisters, with respect and regard for each other's feelings. Philias in a marriage ideally will create an environment of comfort and support that will smooth out the edges in the relationship. Having brotherly and sisterly love for each other makes it easier to get along and cover each other's backs. It sets up the pathway in a marriage for the long haul, and solidifies the marriage in a growing and working relationship.

Eros

Eros has a mythical connotation. Wikipedia tells us that its origin is found in Greek literature. *The Iliad*, by Homer, used the word eros as a common noun meaning sexual desire. The Romans borrowed that connotation from the Greeks and used it to name their god of sexual love, Cupid.

In the context of marriage, eros is love at first sight brought about by the physical and biological need to propagate. It is hormone driven by the biological clock. It is a physical attraction that manifests from thoughts and desires into real sexual acts of making love. Love is eros in the physical act of propagation, the physical act of love that God has created for a man and his wife. Making love in a marriage is paramount in God's creation; marriages are consummated and the couple cleaves as one (Gen. 2:24). In the eyesight of God and in marriage, the physical act of love is holy and acceptable for the couple and for their future in holy living.

It is important to note that, within the confines of marriage, sexual love is important and encouraged by God. When it goes outside of marriage, it defiles itself and brings about estrangement, disharmonies, and sin, as in the sin of adultery (Matt. 5:28). Any act or thoughts by a member of either gender outside of marriage constitutes an act of adultery. God knows all and sees all.

It is important to enjoy your partner in the sacred holiness of marriage. One should not defile it with outside trash like movies or pornography or sexting or texting or social media. Even older couples in their marriage should adhere to Proverbs 5:18–19.

Storge

Storge (pronounced stōr-gā) is the type of love that is expressed between parents and children. Wikipedia describes it as the effective love of family—mother, father, brother, sister, and so on to include all kinfolk. Storge, in the context of marriage, goes into extended families—even the in-laws. Yes, I said it. Storge may be the continuation of your love for your spouse manifested in love for the family you have married into. This demonstration of love means showing love for the mother and father of the person you married.

Why should you love them? Christ first loved you, and you love your spouse. Your love for your mate should transcend the marital relationship to include the family you married into. Accept the family

21

respectfully, with love and appreciation, simply because that is where the love of your life came from. You should love them too.

This love and acceptance may be displayed through warm and friendly gestures of openness at family gatherings, and should include praying regularly for members of the extended family. Let them know that you really care. God knows your heart, so show love for your family members and extended relatives on both sides of the family tree. The more you show love and respect for the parents and relatives of your spouse, the more the favor of the Lord will be a part of you and bless you. The beauty of our living God is in our hearts, so keep on loving and praying and God will continue to smile on your marriage.

Agape

Agape is a Greek term that means love for one another. In Wikipedia sources it is further described as having unselfish, unconditional love for one another. Agape is free from feeling. This type of love is sacrificial; it comes from your very soul. Agape, by choice, suffers inconveniences, discomfort, and even death for the benefit of another without expecting anything in return. This love is the greatest type of love.

Agape, which is voluntary love, goes beyond the other types discussed in that it represents the highest type of love anyone could possibly demonstrate. It is essentially the love of God and His followers as His children. Our walk with Him is a walk with Christ. He paid the ultimate price, which was that He laid down His life so we would be forgiven of our sins and live with Him and the Father forever and ever. Agape is having the love of Jesus in your heart and using Him as the best example of how to love in His kingdom (Eph. 5:1–2).

Please note that we cannot love God without loving our brother and sisters who also love Him. This type of love is all tied together by the Commandments (see Matt. 22:37–40 and Luke 10: 25–28).

In the context of holy matrimony, look back to our first chapter. To find peace and harmony in your marriage, you first must find harmony with God. The love of God and love for God is the epitome of life itself. When you take agape into a marriage in which both spouses are believers, God will oversee and find favor in that marriage.

The manifestation of love will grow in marriage from the feeling of love at first sight to a growing transitional love. As marriages begin to grow and couples encounter different experiences, love becomes transitional, from eros to philia to storge. Agape is the highest type of love to achieve and have. It is Christlike love, sanctified as the highest love we are all trying to achieve. In other words, it is a work in progress that we are constantly striving for.

Manifestations of Love

1. Intimacy

Intimacy, as defined by Webster, is intrinsic; innermost; marked by very close association, contact or familiarity; marked by warm friendship; suggesting informal warmth or privacy.

In the context of Christian marriage, intimacy is framed through prayer for loved ones, and is an avenue or extension of love. An intimate interaction exists between you and God and the loved ones you pray for. Intimacy is a medium of expression that connects a man to his wife, parents to their children, and in-laws to their extended families. Intimacy, to be effective, needs to be a two-way channel, a back-and-forth interaction.

Other forms of intimacy involve aspects of physical interaction that can include spending special time with each other, holding hands, touching lovingly, looking into each other's eyes, walking on the beach, picnicking at the lake, enjoying an ice cream cone together, helping to wash the dishes after a meal, planting flowers, leaving love notes for your mate, or calling your spouse just to say "I'm thinking about you" and "I love you" when you are away from each other. Intimacy is letting your spouse know that you are in it for the long haul, enduring all of the day-to-day hills and valleys of marriage. In other words, intimacy is romancing your spouse. It is a continuation of the honeymoon, maintaining your garden of Eden.

In a web article about intimacy, H. Norman Wright asserts that intimacy is a very strong personal relationship—a special emotional closeness that includes understanding and being understood by someone who is very special. Intimacy has also been defined as an affectionate bond, the strands of which are composed of mutual caring, responsibility, trust, open communication of feelings and sensations, and the non-defended exchange of information about significant emotional events. Intimacy means taking the risk to be close to someone and allowing that someone to step inside your personal boundaries.

Then we come to spiritual intimacy. In the book *The Spiritually Intimate Marriage*, Don Harvey states the most complete definition of spiritual intimacy that I have found. He says spiritual intimacy is "being able to share your spiritual self, find this reciprocated, and have a sense of union with your mate." Spiritual intimacy maintains the closeness to God that also keeps the married couple close to each other and in alignment with God.

How close are you to your spouse? How much time do you invest in the development of spiritual intimacy? How willing are you to adjust your schedules and mentally commit to the process in return for the special closeness and understanding you will build with the one person who is so special to you?

2. Song of Solomon

It is interesting to observe that ministers of faith seem to avoid preaching from the book of the Song of Solomon. Only a few will attempt that avenue to express love. Written by Solomon, according to Jewish tradition, the book expresses the courtship behavior of a man and a woman seeking union in marriage. There are vivid metaphors that describe strong physical feelings that may be too graphic or too vivid for some readers, but the writings are all written in the context of holy matrimony as Adam and Eve lived it in the garden of Eden prior to the Fall. The strong feelings the man and woman have increase their desire to love and to be together.

One thing we must remember and understand is that God created sex and intimacy. They are holy and good when enjoyed in the context of marriage. When sex or even the thought of sex is implicated outside of the covenant of marriage, it becomes defiled. Stay focused on your partner in love and marriage, because God gives you all you need.

Some scholars have described the Song of Solomon as an allegory of the love expressed by God for Israel and the love expressed by Jesus Christ for the church. We know that God so loved the world that He gave us His only Son, Jesus Christ. Jesus Christ loved us so much that He laid down His life in a brutal way to save us from our sins. That in itself is incomprehensible. We must keep the love of God and Christ in our hearts, and keep the love of our spouses also in our hearts. This enables us to stay in alignment with God.

Townsend's Transitional Scale of Love in Christian Marriage

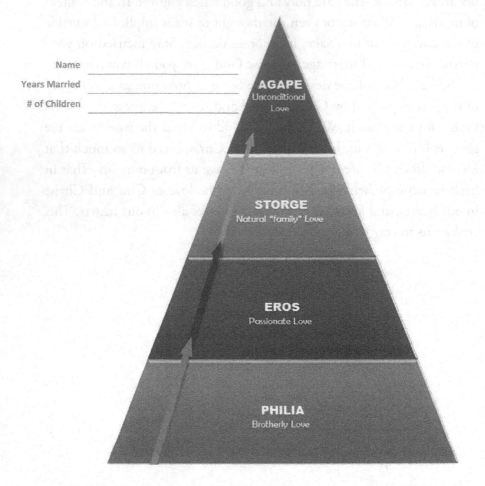

Name _____

Years Married _____

# of Children _____

AGAPE
Unconditional Love

STORGE
Natural "family" Love

EROS
Passionate Love

PHILIA
Brotherly Love

Rate yourself in marriage (in narrative form) based on the type of loves discussed. Pleas make note of the Harmonies in marriage with God, Self, Others and Nature

Chapter 5 Outline

Expectations of Marriage (Maslow's Levels of Needs)

A. Wealth and Money
B. Houses and Cars
C. Children
D. Social Status
E. Biological Model (Natural Selection)

References

Psalm 103:2–5; Psalms 121; Matthew 6:33–34; Ephesians 5:22–24, 33; Colossians 3:17–25; Titus 2:1–7; 1 Timothy 2:9–12; Genesis 3:15; 1 Peter 3:1–6; Proverbs 31:26; 1 Corinthians 11:13; Luke 2:51; Ephesians 5:21; 1 Peter 5:5; Hebrews 13:17; Genesis 12:1–3, 2:18

Discussion

One's expectations of marriage may be delusional due to the euphoric state that love pulls us into. By keeping it real, the expectations are grounded. In the day-to-day demands of life, in other words, what you see is what you get. Deal with it. This chapter explores expectations of marriage. Once the vows have been stated, the deal is sealed. Then the process begins. Marriage becomes a plan and a work in progress, moving toward certain goals and higher expectations. Where do you and your spouse want to be? The stages of life and of marriage are great realistic indicators based on your individual needs and progression in life.

Objectives

Upon review of this chapter, the participants will achieve the following objectives:

1. Reexamine their expectations of marriage and determine if they are in line with God's plan and also with their desires for marriage
2. Review Maslow's levels of needs and contrast them with their own levels of needs in their Christian walk and marriage
3. List scripture passages relating to God's promises to fulfill all our needs and expectations

Questions

1. What are your expectations for your marriage? Do they align with God's plan for marriage?
2. Do your needs in marriage compare or contrast with Maslow's levels of needs?

CHAPTER 5

Expectations of Marriage
(Maslow's Levels of Needs)

This chapter contrasts Maslow's levels of needs to living a Christian marriage. Maslow's levels of needs are a socioeconomic theory based on assessment of individuals' goals and needs. They are in fact, associated with levels of existence in the social strata of our culture. The theorist asserts that this scale, and your level on it, bears an intrinsic value to us as humans—an inward desire to improve one's position in life. Regardless of the level you find yourself on, all people have that intrinsic motivation to improve their quality of life by moving up the scale. The higher one moves up the scale, the more one feels good about oneself—a greater sense of self-worth. One then will have a greater tendency to reach out to help others.

Maslow asserts that there is an intrinsic motivation in all humans to respond in this manner. The higher one moves up in society, the more one reaches out and does more for society. This builds a greater sense of self-gratification, resulting in what Maslow calls "self-actualization" needs. His premise is that self-actualization needs are the highest type of social need. His scale goes from the lowest level, physiological, to safety, to love and belonging, to esteem, and then to the highest level, self-actualization.

In the context of holy matrimony, for Christians in a postmodern society, the question comes to mind, "Where are we situated?" Where are we if we have bought in to Maslow's theory? Where are we as married Christians on his grand scale of actualization? Let us consider where we are in our marriages. Consider the stages of marriage. Are we newlyweds, honeymooners, young families, families with preteens and teenagers, empty nesters, couples who are taking care of elderly parents? All of these things should be considered when assessing one's level of self-actualization.

Maslow's hierarchy is based on the needs of the self. It is solely "in the flesh." Each level of the scale exhibits things that make one feel that all one's basic needs are met. I feel safe, loved, secure, and self-actualized; I am in the position that I can give to those in need. But am I really self-actualized based on the fact that I have food, clothing, and shelter that I bought? Am I self-actualized if I am in a safe environment that I constructed with security systems, alarm systems, and gated fences around my community? Am I self-actualized because I have money in great banks? Am I self-actualized because I am a philanthropist, putting money into foundations and scholarships? Am I self-actualized because my name is written on towers in great American cities? All these things are good, but without Christ, what does it all really mean?

If we confess that Jesus Christ is Lord, Master, and Savior of this universe and that He died for our sins, then we are truly self-actualized through the love of Jesus Christ.

Maslow's theory, in the context of holy matrimony, does not fit. There is incongruence. Psalm 121 tells us that God will meet all of our needs day and night, season by season. Regardless of the phase your marriage is in, if God is in your life, all your needs will be met. Maslow's scale is based upon man's interaction with man, which is cardinal. Maslow's emphasis is on dealing in the flesh. The Christian concept in holy matrimony is that God is always with you from the moment you say, "I do." In Genesis 12:1–3, the covenant between God and Abraham and all who believe states that "I will Bless thee ... so that you will be a blessing ... and by all the families of the earth shall bless themselves."

The key isn't a matter of struggling through the stages of Maslow's hierarchy. Blessed by the grace of God, you are "thriving through" life and celebrating God's goodness at all levels because Jesus is making it happen. God is with you in all aspects of your marital journey.

This is not to say that you should not have ambitions. God wants us to strive and be successful. However, be sure to put God first.

In addition to the expectations, we each have of marriage that are relevant to Maslow's hierarchy—things that are tangible and materialistic, sociological and physiological—we should also look at what is expected of us according to God's Word. For married couples united in the sight of God, there are certain things that are expected of the wife and also of the husband, individually and collectively. Basic needs can be pretty easily met. There are more expectations of each partner that should be discussed. These expectations are complementary responsibilities to both marriage partners.

For the wife, the greatest expectation of her is submission or support. For the husband, the greatest expectation is leadership as head of the household and lover of his wife and family. (See Eph. 5:22–24, 33; Col. 3:17–25; Titus 2:1–7; 1 Tim. 2:12; Gen. 3:15; 1 Pet. 3:1–6.) These scripture passages show us that submission is required of both parties.

Submission and support by the wife must be clearly defined and understood. First let us look at what submission is not. Submission doesn't mean that a wife is a footstool to her husband, running to answer his every beck and call. According to Proverbs 31:10–31, the ideal or virtuous woman is trusted by her husband because he is assured that her intentions toward him are all good, not evil. Everything she does, she does willingly. She cares willingly because of her love for him. She sees the needs of her husband, her family, and all others around her. She instills pride and confidence in her husband when he is in the presence of his peers and older men. Through her support of her husband, she submits to the will of God. Submission doesn't mean that she cannot speak when she has an opinion. She can offer wise advice (Prov. 31:26, Acts 18:26) and knowledge with kindness. Submission does not mean a wife cannot exhibit her God-given talents and abilities (Prov. 31). Instead, she uses her talents to provide for the household in a way that brings comfort, income, beauty, and honor to her husband and children.

Submission and support do not mean that the wife is inferior to her husband. Her position with God simply puts her in alignment after her husband because God has declared the husband to be the head of the household. This is God's order (1 Cor. 11:13). It can be compared to Jesus's position vis-à-vis God: Jesus is head of the church as man is head of the household.

Submission and support are not concepts for women only. They are concepts for all who believe in God (see Eph. 5:21; 1 Pet. 5:5; Heb. 13:17). These scripture passages make clear God's insistence on order and the division of responsibilities, which will shift and change over time as one goes through life's phases.

Marriage can get to a point where you enter a "woulda, coulda, shoulda" phase after the children have grown and left the house. The couple begins to reflect on things and see how they could or should have done those things differently. The spouses start blaming each other for mistakes made. Couples should realize that this is the devil's way of entering into the marriage, causing conflict and disharmonies. Please note that you cannot undo the past, but you can change and build a greater and stronger marital relationship through Jesus Christ as your Savior.

So, what can a married couple expect when the wife chooses to be submissive to and supportive of her husband? They can expect an attitude of willingness to be there for each other. They can expect to be a team, in which the wife uses her talents and gifts for the greater good of the marriage. With the husband as head of the household, the wife can still expect to have the freedom and love to be creative and contribute to the marriage while ensuring, through loyalty and love, that she will not do anything detrimental to the marriage.

The husband, as leader and lover, provides the basic needs, security, and love for his wife and family only through obedience and the love of Jesus Christ. The husband, being designated by God as head of the home, becomes a servant of God and the greater servant of his family. His role model is Jesus the Christ, who came not to be served, but to serve. Keeping his wife and family's best interest at heart, the husband has the responsibility of being a frequent companion to his wife in the home. In addition, he is to be his wife's teacher and set a good example for his family. His life should be exemplary in order to earn their respect and his authority in the home (see Phil. 4:9; 1 Thess. 2:7–10; 1 Pet. 5:3). An exemplary life is not easily achieved, due to man's nature. It is something he must constantly strive for. When he fails, it is important that he confesses his failures to God and his wife and ask for forgiveness, as an example to his mate.

As head of the household, the man is responsible to ensure that work gets done. He will listen to the counsel of his wife and respect her advice as his partner in marital decisions.

The husband is expected to be his wife's lover. He must love her as he loves himself. His love for her is compared to Christ's love for the church. It cannot be measured. It is unconditional and sacrificial by choice.

A husband's love is shown through his devotion to his wife and family, providing for their safety and well-being at all times (Eph.5:28). He prays for his wife and family. He expresses his love for his wife through words and by satisfying her various needs—physical, emotional, intellectual, and social (1 Tim. 5:8; 1 John 3:17; Eph. 5:28). He helps her with household chores and the children. The husband will make sacrifices for his wife and family, doing things he really doesn't feel like doing or when he would rather be doing something else. He will attend his daughter's piano recital when he would rather be watching a football game, or go to a family gathering with his in-laws when he'd rather catch up on some much-needed rest (Eph. 5:25; Phil. 2:5–6). He will share things like feelings, dreams and ideas with his wife, drawing the couple closer together (1 Pet. 3:7).

If the husband can express to his wife that next to God, she is first in his life—before his work, before the children, before their parents—she will feel secure in the marriage relationship. The husband is expected to praise and show respect for his wife (1 Pet. 3:7; Prov. 31:27–28).

Each partner should examine themselves to determine if they are meeting God's expectations in their marriage. Even if they know what is expected of them, are they applying it to their marriage relationship? If not, they must confess these things to God and to their spouse. Seek repentance (Eph. 1:7) and ask to be changed by the Holy Spirit (Gal. 5:16, 22, 23). Make the changes necessary to become obedient to God in order to promote oneness in marriage (Phil. 2:12–13; James 1:19–24).

In summary, one's expectations of marriage may fall within the realm of Maslow's hierarchy of needs. However, we are instructed to look to God first in all that we do. "Trust in the Lord with all thine heart; and lean not unto thine own understanding. In all thy ways acknowledge Him, and He shall direct thy paths" (Prov. 3:5–6) KJV. All your expectations and needs will be provided within the will of God (Ps. 23).

Our expectations for marriage should not include the simple expectation that the husband's job is to be leader, lover, and maker of the rules. Neither should we expect the wife to be only supportive and submissive to her husband, seeing to it that his rules are followed. Our expectations in marriage should be all-encompassing. God has proclaimed that we should help each other to become one in the sight of God and to achieve goals in a life of endless opportunity, to be shared and enjoyed by both partners.

Marriage is indeed a work in progress at all levels, from starting out as newlyweds to seeing the children through college. The good news is, once you become a believer in Christ and a born-again Christian, you and your mate are automatically self-actualized through the love, grace, and mercy of Jesus Christ. Regardless of what stage you are in marriage, God is blessing you so that you can be a blessing to others. In regards to wealth, children, and social status, God will make it all happen as He sees fit in His own time (Eccles. 3:1–12). By being self-actualized in Christ, wherever you work or whatever position you hold, God will bless you, and you will be able to bless others at work and in the community. These blessings are continued in the home environment, where God will bless your family as long as you keep Christ in the center of your daily life. God wants you to have things and achieve success.

It is important to know that all of the things you achieve in marriage are owed to God, who makes it all happen.

MASLOW'S HIERCHY OF NEEDS

Name_____

Years Married_____

Number of Children_____

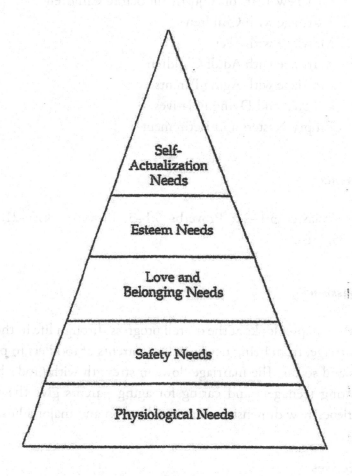

Rate yourself in marriage (in narrative form) based on the type of needs discussed.

Chapter 6 Outline

Stages of Marriage

    A. Honeymoon
    B. First Few Years of Adjustment before Children
    C. Marriage with Children
    D. Marriage with Teens
    E. Marriage with Adult Children
    F. Marriage with Aging Parents
        a. Sick and Dying Relatives
    B. Empty Nesters and Retirement

References

    Ecclesiastes 3:1–22; Proverbs 5:1–3; Proverbs 8:13–21, 3:1–13, 6:16–35, 7:1–2

Discussion

    This chapter looks at the overall progress through life in the process of marriage, from being newlyweds to parents of toddlers to parents of teens and so on. The marriage flows in strength with God's blessings. Parenting teenagers and caring for aging parents give the marriage experience new dimensions for consideration and major adjustments.

Objectives

    Upon review of this chapter, the participants will achieve the following objectives:

    1. Reflect on the honeymoon and early years of adjustment in marriage

2. Identify their Christian walk in their stage of marriage
3. Reflect on past stages where they might have taken a different approach
4. Correlate their Christian walk in all stages of marriage as outlined

Questions

1. How does your honeymoon stage compare with where you are in marriage now?
2. Beyond the honeymoon, what has been your most memorable stage of marriage so far?
3. In reflection, what stage of marriage would you like to revisit and perhaps modify?

CHAPTER 6

Stages of Marriage

The honeymoon stage of marriage is the period of several weeks after you say, "I do." In some cases, the honeymoon may extend to the point when the children are born. This is a period of adjustment to marriage. It is experiencing the new feeling of having to be responsible to another living soul, your husband or wife. Everything you do and say is a reflection on you and your mate.

At this time, a sense of oneness comes into play. You get and do things together. You bond with unified commitment of mutual indebtedness.

Marriage is further solidified with the birth of the first child and then more children. Commitment is real and important when you think of a spouse and children dependent on you. If you are yoked together and have God in your lives, your children are extended blessings from God.

In a Christian marriage that includes raising children, it is important that you and your mate agree on the discipline of your children. Children need to learn that the rules first come from God, from whom all blessings flow. It is important to pray as a family and teach children to pray alone too. This will add harmony to the household.

Children's teen years, in most cases, are the most difficult years of a marriage. Outside influences weigh heavily on the harmonious environment of the home. These outside influences come mostly from the peer groups that teens identify with to stay cool or popular.

Church-related activities are good for youth to indulge in. Such activities help to ensure that the peer group is like-minded in their understanding of living their lives with God and Christ. A church-active Christian family is a marriage that God oversees with divine intervention and protection. God smiles upon the marriage because, as He states, "Train up a child in the way he should go; and when he is old, he will not depart from it" (Prov. 22:6) KJV A church-active family is one in which the father has an active role in the church, the mother has a role in the church, and all of the children are members of different church groups or ministries. The family has a connection to the church and duties connected to their spiritual gifts. Their gifts are developmental, along the lines of spiritual growth in living a life pleasing to God. Everyone in the family contributes to the church and serves to some extent. In the church, there are like-minded Christian families to meet and connect with to create a wholesome Christian network of families who are believers. This helps to strengthen the marriage, the family, and the Christian community.

When the children leave the home for college, the military, or adult life in the world, then you and your spouse become empty nesters. In some cases, you have to become reacquainted with your mate and their uniqueness, and reconfigure the marriage all over again. This is a very sensitive period. Married partners begin to redefine themselves. Support for each other's true feelings is delicate and real and extremely important. You and your spouse are facing the retirement phase and dealing with adult children. This phase of marriage brings about new challenges. You and your spouse find that you have more time for each other. You realize each of you has grown and changed. This is a time for reacquaintance and renewal of the friendship you had earlier on.

The empty nest time may be a time to refocus on the marriage and explore new and special events together without the constraints of schedules and budgets as you knew them while raising children. This is a time when you can take a fresh look at your well-being as mature adults. Physical, emotional, and spiritual well-being may be examined as you prepare for the rest of your lives together. You may experience a new sense of purpose, togetherness, and spiritual intimacy in your marriage, which should forever include the presence of the Holy Spirit in all that you do as husband and wife.

The next phase includes caring for elderly, sick, and dying parents. All of the love and support from each side of the marriage is necessary to make sure one's marriage partner is not being left alone in their worries and sorrows. This is done by your physical presence and support of them at the hospital or nursing home during their illness, surgeries and at the time of their passing. Faith in God and belief in Christ as a couple will help you through troubling times with aging and dying parents. Agape and storge are greatly needed during this time of your married relationship.

To ensure a strong and lengthy marriage, continue to pray for each other and continue to pray together. When you pray through all the challenges that life can bring in each stage of marriage, you will find that your faith grows and your walk with God deepens.

Chapter 7 Outline

Fulfilling the Needs of Marriage

    A. Emotional, Physical, and Psychological
    B. Self-Efficacy and Self Esteem
    C. Security and Contentment

References

    2 Corinthians 6:1–14; Ephesians 5:2–25, 33; 1 Corinthians 13:4–8; 1 Corinthians 7:1–6; Hebrews 13:4; Matthew 5:11

Discussion

    This chapter is based on the needs of both spouses. In the progression of a marriage, various needs will come and go for each partner. The reason why such needs vary in both genders is because of our biological clocks. The clock is forever ticking away. Our needs in marriage address career, children, and preparation for retirement. All this can catch us up in a quagmire of emotions. This chapter will address these issues from a biblical perspective, leading to the justification of marriage.

Objectives

    Upon review of this chapter, the participants will achieve the following objectives:

    1. Identify in your marriage, emotional and psychological needs that have been met in your marriage
    2. List how psychological and emotional needs have enhanced your marriage if they have been met

3. Explain how justification in Christ is also justification in marriage
4. Explain how your biological equivalent has satisfied your needs beyond the physical
5. Explain what impact your marriage has had on your self-efficacy and self-esteem

Questions

1. Beyond the physical, what other needs have been met in your marriage?
2. What has marriage done to your self-image, if anything?
3. What level of dependency do you feel your marriage is in?

CHAPTER 7

Fulfilling the Needs of Marriage

There are various needs expressed in a Christian marriage that should be met or reconciled by both parties, husband and wife, when the time presents itself. The most obvious is the physical need for sexual satisfaction, followed by emotional and psychological needs.

Having a healthy and strong sexual relationship in marriage enables both husband and wife to be satisfied beyond the physical need. The demonstration of love manifested in the physical act reassures both partners of their spouse's love and caring. Physical needs, when met, add to the validation of emotional needs—that my spouse really loves me.

Follow-up on other needs is a constant work in progress. We suggest that married couples keep their antennas and GPS systems up and be sensitive to the changing emotions of their partners. Over the years of marriage, initial needs are slowly replaced by other needs. For example, a new expression of need may be the need to start a family. The time to start a family must be agreed upon by both parties, just like both parties must agree on other joint activities, major purchases, and so on. It is important that both of you desire to start a family.

When both spouses are in agreement, it makes for a very happy pregnancy, leading to happy children. Why happy children? Because even in pregnancy, the developing child in all stages feels the love of both partners. This brings about a happy family, full of love and sharing in God's blessings.

The need to be a parent is intrinsic and biological. It is very fulfilling, both emotionally and psychologically, because, in a sense, it validates our existence on earth. To be a father or a mother is God's way of letting couples fulfill God's earthly domain. God wants us to reproduce and have children. When both partners don't agree upon the need to start a family, tension may exist during and after the pregnancy, and the child may feel the tension between parents in their early stages of life.

Marriage is a roller coaster, full of ups and downs, good times and bad times. Partners in marriage need to be cognizant of the day-to-day emotions of their spouses. Support and communication are important in all phases of marriage. Let your mate know what you are going through. Be right there with your partner all the way, reassuring and comforting them.

Improvements in self-image, in marriage and in life, can be discovered by getting more education or training. These are pivotal decisions that the married couple should discuss. The desire to get a better job during marriage may be a complicated thing. There are risks involved, and each partner must be on board for the big change. This change, although temporary, may cause uncomfortable adjustments that turn your routine upside down. When one spouse goes to school at night, the other must take care of the children, help with homework, and fix meals.

The key here is to stay focused on the goal of improving the lives of the student spouse and the family. In the long run, these adjustments are good for the family as a whole. Take everything to God in prayer together. God knows your heart. God knows your needs even before you thought you had them. He will see you through in all that you do. Please keep Him first.

Improving oneself by obtaining an education automatically elevates one's self-esteem and self-image. It also elevates the family self-image. Regardless of how high you rise in society, please stay grounded in the Lord. To God be the glory, because He has made it all happen.

Satisfying the needs of both spouses in marriage is a lifelong process. Needs will change over time and will depend on the stages of the marriage. With good communication and constant prayer, the marriage can be both fulfilling and satisfying.

We have explored the expectations couples might have in their marriages, and we have compared and contrasted these expectations with God's expectations for marriage. We have also looked at how these expectations play out in the different stages of marriage. It is important to note that God's plan and purpose for marriage is completely justified in the biological realm of "be fruitful and multiply" (Gen. 1:28) KJV. It is also justified in terms of the love God wants us to have for each other. Marriage encompasses all types of love throughout the cycle of life.

Whether marital needs are emotional, physical, or psychological, they can be met through prayer and trust in the Lord. Your advantage is in being equally yoked. From this you can develop the spiritual intimacy that will lead to fulfillment (2 Cor. 6:14–15).

Prayer in marriage should be deliberate, unified, purposeful, and mutual for spiritual bonding. Satisfaction of the needs of both partners at each stage of the marriage will require a commitment by both parties to smooth out differences and keep the marriage strong. Nothing about marriage should be taken for granted. Unexpected realities of life must be faced head on and worked through so you can grow together, with God in the midst of it. Remember, you are each unique within yourselves. Patience is a requirement.

Finding and keeping friendship in the marriage union is important. Exhibiting caring and forgiveness and maintaining a sense of maturity prevents feelings of resentment and hostility from entering your domain. Spending time alone together helps nurture your marriage and reminds you of why you married. Supporting each other's interests and lifting each other up when a partner is down helps the marriage to thrive. Satisfaction can be found by exercising the fruits of the Spirit and being mindful at all times of your partner.

Marriage is a work in progress. Expectations may not be satisfied when we want or in the manner that we may want. Sometimes we have to wait on God.

Chapter 8 Outline

Gender Roles and Responsibilities in Marriage

A. Role of the Husband
B. Role of the Wife
C. Traditional and Nontraditional Roles
D. Maintaining a Good Spiritual Life in Marriage

References

Genesis 2:18–25; Proverbs 31:10–31; 1 Peter 3:1–7; Ephesians 5:21–33; Romans 12:10, 13:8; Ephesians 4:2, 31–32

Discussion

This chapter discusses the roles and responsibilities of the man and the woman in a marriage situation. Traditional roles that are still practiced lend clarity to Bible teachings. Other roles may vary based on the changing dynamics of our culture, such as who has the best job or can do more to support the family. How these dynamics may or may not affect marriage in the Christian household will be explored.

Objectives

Upon review of this chapter, the participants will achieve the following objectives:

1. List five main responsibilities of husbands and wives based upon the stage of your marriage
2. Explain blended roles as they apply to marriage
3. Discuss submission and its impact on marriage

4. Identify irresponsibility in marriage and correlate it with your needs
5. Discuss the evolution of families, marriage, and the rights of women in postmodern American culture

Questions

1. What roles should a man and a woman in marriage follow today?
2. What are your views of stay-at-home moms and dads?
3. Will we ever go back to traditional roles in marriage in our society?
4. What has American history taught us in regard to the roles we play?

CHAPTER 8

Gender Roles and Responsibilities in Marriage

In considering gender and the role each gender plays in a marriage that is Christ-centered, we focus on three types of marriage that are common in our experience: traditional, survival mode, and open.

Traditional roles in marriage are the type that fall in the category of "natural," based on two genders, male and female. In a traditional marriage, the man has specific duties and the female has her duties. These roles are readily adopted in most contemporary cultures. The man is the main breadwinner and makes sure the physical needs of the household are met, for the most part. He makes sure the home is a safe environment. The decisions stop with him. He is head of the household as Christ is head of the church.

Traditional roles may shift when conditions of life change the family dynamics. The loss of a job may require that the wife take up the slack and go to work, for example. The question is, "To what degree does this change the dynamics of the family structure, if at all?" The man has to function in a different role. It may be temporary. Then the family structure may have to adjust to what we call "survival mode," which means just getting through the current problem that won't last forever. Regardless of whether the adjustment is temporary or long range, the role of the man is important in holding on to the family structure. The man should have the final word on the direction of the family when the wife consents to follow, but both should go to God first before deciding what to do.

Throughout life, certain health and physical problems may become factors in the roles we play in marriage. The roles again must be adjusted in order to maintain a good marriage. Couples over time will transcend a committed relationship and become devoted. When does this type of relationship transpire? You will never know exactly when, but you will know you are in the process. That is the beauty of love and marriage.

Why is it important that both partners go to God in the decision-making process? The transition from a committed relationship to a devoted relationship is the manifestation of love that partners declare in their wedding vows in the eyes of God. Nontraditional roles in marriage may be allowed by God, but not sanctioned by God. If God is in the midst, the marriage will go on, and different situations will be tolerated by both partners in order to keep the marriage together and sustain its growth and development. Role reversal is common, for the most part, when constant adjustments in day-to-day activities are required to make the marriage run smoothly.

Open marriage is the type of marriage in which vows are disregarded and partners do what they want, including seeing other people outside of marriage. Marriage as a sacred institution is defiled in this case. This is not sanctioned by God. Such a marriage leaves an open door for sin and sorrow, leading to a breakdown in what the structure of marriage is all about. Such marriages do not engage in having children and building family. This type of arrangement is totally outside of the church. Hence, it is nothing but marriage in sin, if it is marriage at all.

The roles and responsibilities of marriage should never be set as permanent fixtures. Only the relative positions of the partners should be permanent. That is, the husband is head of the household in alignment after Christ, and the wife is in the position after the husband, followed by the children. No matter what the husband does—whether he works or not, whether he takes care of the home, cooks, and cares for the children while his wife works—he should always remain the head of the household, as Christ is the head of the church. A husband may take on the traditional duties that a wife usually performs, but according to scripture, his wife is still the helpmate to him.

It sometimes happens, even after the husband resumes employment, that he may decide to continue to perform traditionally wifely chores, especially if his wife continues to work outside the home. When a married couple goes through times like this, the husband realizes the virtue of his wife—the support she gives, the good she does for the family, and the trust her husband can have in her to be there even in difficult times.

Likewise, the wife sees the heart of her husband and the pain he endures for his family. She is determined to support him and encourage him until he gets back on his feet. This may be the transcending moment when the commitment made at the wedding altar becomes the devoted, loyal relationship that the couple shares forever.

Scripture reminds us that the wife must honor and be in subjection to the husband (Eph. 5:22–24). This means in all circumstances. Life situations change, and when they do, we have to pull together and do whatever it takes to get through those times together. If the married couple can be flexible in their roles and responsibilities, especially when there are children in the marriage, the difficult times become easier to bear.

It is particularly important for married partners to trade off and share roles and responsibilities when children are involved. In blended families and marriages with children, the roles shift constantly because of changes in schedules. Family members' activities demand a sharing of duties in order to fulfill the commitments we make to school, church, community, and family. None of these role changes diminish or change the fact that Dad is still head of the home and Mom is still his helpmate. When children see that their parents are willing to share responsibilities and help each other get through situations, they learn about duty and love. Children see that working things out together, no matter who does what, shows love and affection while keeping the unity of the Spirit in the bond of peace in marriage (Eph. 4:2–4).

Chapter 9 Outline

Communication in Marriage

    A. Long- and Short-Range Goals in Marriage
    B. Verbal Communication
    C. Nonverbal Communication
        1. Body Language
        2. Written Language
    D. Openness and Honesty
    E. Check Your Attitude
    F. Control the Tongue
    G. Listen

References

Amos 3:3; Ephesians 4:24–32; 1 John 1:7–10; James 1:26, 3:5–13; 1 Corinthians 13:1–8; Proverbs 4:23–25

Discussion

This chapter focuses on communication in marriage as it relates to various personalities and how spouses communicate with each other. Behavior modification is necessary to cope with problems and concerns that arise in the marriage. Both partners need to be aware of behavior adjustments they can make in problematic situations, for improvement's sake. This is where openness and honesty come into play.

Objectives

Upon review of this chapter, the participants will achieve the following objectives:

1. Describe different situations in which communication can break down in a marriage
2. List nonverbal traits that are often observed in your spouse's behavior, leading to a breakdown in communication
3. Make note of indicators of personality traits that lead to communication problems in a marriage
4. Describe the various modes of verbal and nonverbal communication that may have a positive or negative impact on a marriage
5. Create short-range goals in five-year increments for improving communication in your marriage, up to twenty years out

Questions

1. How can verbal and nonverbal communication traits break down harmony in a marriage?
2. Where is the indicator of guilt that can bring about immediate resolution in a marital problem?
3. How does the tone of your voice determine the outcome of a conflict?
4. List five ways that you have been able to reconcile differences based upon miscommunication.
5. Have you established short- and long-range communication goals? What are they?

Note: See the communication exercise in the appendix.

CHAPTER 9

Communication in Marriage

Communication in marriage is established shortly after the honeymoon period. This is the most difficult thing to adjust to. Living in the new millennium, couples may practice living together even before they say, "I do." (Quite often, they don't!)

Regardless, there are aspects of our personalities that we keep hidden until the commitment is made at the altar and consummation takes place in the marriage. Then the real person comes out. You may find yourself thinking, *Wow! I didn't know my partner liked that. I didn't know my partner was that kind of person. Who did I really marry? The person I said "I do" to was totally different. How can I communicate to my partner about important things that need to be addressed?*

After the ceremony, when real life in marriage begins, it is important to have goals to reach for. Planning is important. Consider short-range goals and long-range goals. Communicate to your partner where you want to be in your marriage five to ten years down the road. Communication keeps couples on the same track to marital success. Plan together on a number of things.

There are several essential matters that can change the dynamics in a marriage. The first is finances. Decide whether to have separate or joint bank accounts. How are the bills to be paid? You must agree on this through good communication. Second, decide whether to buy a house or rent. The third is the biggest one: whether or not to have children.

Good communication and planning are everything in a marriage. Communication and planning keep you together in terms of your direction and the path you will take in the marriage.

Planning in marriage never stops. After children come into the picture, the conversation and planning for their education begins. Is the goal college or technical training or the military? Where will education take place?

When decisions are made over furniture or a new automobile or the university a child will attend, both partners should be in agreement. When things go wrong—and in life's process, things *will* go wrong—you both can say, "We made that mistake," without the blame game of "I told you so." Blame is what adds stress to the marriage. Accusations can cause a spouse to become resentful, and repeated accusations can lead to abusive behavior on either side.

The mechanics of communication are used throughout the course of a marriage. Verbal and nonverbal skills are learned behaviors based on your interactions with your partner through various experiences. By living together for a long time, your personalities will blend. You and your mate will be able to read each other's expressions and be conscious of when one is upset or angry.

Please understand that love must be at the forefront of all decisions and planning. Pray to God first. He will help you overcome the obstacles in life and marriage as you work hard to achieve your goals. When you pray for major goals in your marriage, we suggest you pray together on hands and knees.

Conveying feelings, desires, and needs to each other may require a change in your thought process about marriage. When you were single, your lifestyle and the way you handled your business were completely different. These changes brought about by marriage should not be taken lightly and require both thoughtful consideration and discussion. Perhaps counseling by qualified personnel will clear the air and make things understandable when problems arise. But first, go to God in prayer.

Communication is not just talking to each other. Communication involves body language, expressions, actions, voice tones, listening, and all that is involved in bringing about clarity of meaning. It includes knowing when *not* to talk. Knowing when to hold your tongue can be the hardest communication skill to learn. James 3:5–8 KJV speaks of the "little member" that defiles and is difficult to tame. Psalm 141:3 (KJV) is a prayer from David asking God to "set a watch, O Lord, before my mouth; keep the door of my lips." We all know that once something is said, it can never be retracted. Please remember that in all situations and conflicts. Listen.

Throughout the course of your marriage, you will have many opportunities to practice your communication skills. Perhaps the best way to begin that practice is to 1) remember the Golden Rule and 2) think before you speak.

Chapter 10 Outline

Decision-Making in Marriage

    A. The Husband
    B. The Wife
    C. A Shared Relationship
    D. Children

References

    Ephesians 5:22–33, 1:22; Hebrews 4:16

Discussion

This chapter focuses on decision-making in marriage and the roles and responsibilities that may come into play. Some marriages are arranged so that one spouse makes all the decisions, and in others the spouses share decision-making. Both partners need to be happy in marriage with their arrangement. Marriage is a shared arrangement. The spouses will receive the benefits of decisions in varying degrees and at different times throughout the marriage; however, all family members will benefit in the long run.

Objectives

Upon review of this chapter, the participants will achieve the following objectives:

1. Determine areas of agreement and disagreement with their spouses and come to a healthy conclusion
2. Understand the differences in gender and the role gender plays in the decision-making process in marriage

3. Prepare to compromise in the decision-making process for the good of the marriage
4. Show unity in the decision-making process when it comes to family matters and children

Questions

1. Do you always get to decide what is best?
2. How do you feel about always making hard choices?
3. What are some of the hard choices to be made in marriage?
4. Do you share in decision-making to ensure shared responsibilities?

CHAPTER 10

Decision-Making in Marriage

Decision-making in marriage is an acquired position to which couples adapt beginning soon after the marriage ceremony. Traditionally, the man takes the lead in determining major aspects of both lives. As scripture states in 1 Peter 3, the man is head of his household as Christ is head of the church.

Does this mean that whatever the man decides is right? Let's think about this. Should the man make *all* of the decisions by himself, while his wife follows his decisions regardless? I think not! The husband has his wife as his partner. A partner means there are two who are to be considered in all decisions made in a marriage, from the beginning to the end. This in turn means that the results of your decisions will not only affect you (if you are the man) but also will affect your wife and family.

As a man, and biblically speaking, we hope you would want your wife as well as yourself to be pleased with your decision, seeking a good outcome that is pleasing to both of you. How often does it happen that a decision is made by only one of you, without concessions? Very rarely. Both man and wife, as partners in marriage, must be in agreement throughout the course of the marriage. The wife's point of view is an equal point of view and should be taken seriously in any decision. A husband's decision cannot be selfish or self-gratifying with no thought of the consequences to others. This applies also to the wife. Her decisions will reflect on her husband, for good or ill.

Making decisions can sometimes prove tricky and unpredictable. For instance, in cases where the parents have blended families, decision-making that has to be done immediately can be difficult. It may not be convenient or timely to consult with one's spouse. This requires that one partner make a decision without the approval or knowledge of the other. Each spouse should be able to trust the judgment of their partner to make the best decision for all involved. Trust in the other's judgment must be established as early as possible in the marriage.

Even when you both agree on a decision, the event may not have a good outcome. Use these instances as lessons to cement the marriage, and learn to approach such situations differently in the future. Learn from your mistakes. God has given us freedom to make choices. These freedoms come with limitations, because we are ultimately responsible to God. We must look to Him and rely on Him to help us make good decisions.

Sometimes it may be necessary for both of you to take the problem to God in prayer. Pray alone; then pray together. Lay your burdens down before God, and He will give you directions to move on. Trust in Him in prayer. Make the decisions together, mindful of the impact that the results will have on you and your partner. After prayer, you can be relaxed in your decision, trusting in the Lord. God will make things happen.

> Put not your trust in princes, nor in the son of man, in whom there is no help ... Happy is he that hath the God of Jacob for his help, whose hope is in the Lord his God which made heaven and earth. (Ps. 146:3,5- 6) KJV

> Trust in the Lord with all thine heart; and lean not unto thine own understanding. In all thy ways acknowledge Him, and He shall direct thy paths. (Prov. 3:5-6) KJV

The roles we take on throughout our married lives and the responsibilities that come with those roles often influence the decisions we make. When we feel responsible for certain aspects of the marriage, our decision-making takes on a different perspective. For example, couples with children will choose a very different car to purchase compared to couples who do not have children. Similarly, the thought process about purchasing a home will be very different for a young family compared to one with elderly parents. Similar considerations can affect the way you make decisions about job opportunities or education.

Should married couples make decisions on their own, or should they seek advice from an outside source? There will be many times when couples have difficulty making important decisions. It can be helpful for them to seek advice from wise counsel, who can guide them to the best decision.

Who, however, might be considered "wise counsel"? Do you go to your best friends? Do you confide in your parents? Your pastor? What about a professional, like a financial advisor or a lawyer? Depending on the seriousness of the decision to be made, any of these could be called upon for advice.

Of course, the wisest counsel comes from God, who will guide your path and even lead you to the best person to seek advice from (John 16:13). Prayer is always the best first choice for wise counsel so that you can both be of one mind (1 Pet. 3:8).

Chapter 11 Outline

Commitment

    A. How Much?
    B. How Far?
    C. To Whom?

References

Romans 10:9–10; Acts 16:31; Ephesians 5:20–33; Mark 10:5–9; Proverbs 12:14–28, 31, 10:31; Psalms 128:1–6

Discussion

This chapter explores the depth and breadth of the obligation of spouses to each other. How true will they be to the vows they stated in holy matrimony?

Objectives

Upon review of this chapter, the participants will achieve the following objectives:

1. Determine how much of a commitment the husband will pledge to the marriage
2. Determine how much of a commitment the wife will pledge to the marriage
3. Determine how much of a commitment both spouses will pledge to the marriage
4. Determine factors that test marital commitment and list them

Questions

1. Husbands, how much are you committed to your marriage?
2. Wives, how much are you committed to your marriage?
3. What do you as a husband feel you are committed to in marriage?
4. What do you as a wife feel you are committed to in marriage?
5. What are gender variations in commitment within the contemporary marriage?

CHAPTER 11

Commitment

Commitment is the most difficult aspect of marriage. It is the cement of the marriage, a covenant to each other. It is a vow to be committed to that other person *for life*.

Variations of the love theme determine commitment, depending on whether it is philia, eros, storge, or agape. Commitment of a husband to his wife and of a father to his children is based on the needs of each person within the relationship. It can extend to in-laws. A husband will take on two and even three jobs if necessary, to support family, with the support of his wife. His commitment is first of all to God, from whom all blessings flow. He is committed to his household as Christ is head of the church.

Commitment is demanding and arduous. It requires perseverance and steadfastness, all pointing to goals in life. Commitment in marriage is stepping out on faith—not knowing the outcome, but trusting in God. It is seeking trust in yourself to do God's will, regardless of all obstacles, trials, and tribulations. Trust in God. He will see you through.

Through commitment, you become a devoted husband, father, Christian, and family man.

When you and your spouse decided to take that big step and exchange the vows of marriage, how much time did you spend thinking about commitment—commitment to your partner, to marriage, and to all that marriage entails? Some people spend quite a bit of time pondering this commitment before they ask for and accept the marriage bond. Others never give it a thought. They just dive right in with both feet!

Serious thinkers who have faith in God and His plans for our lives think about commitment in almost everything we do. In every aspect of our lives, commitment is serious business.

What are some of the things you are committed to—your walk with God, your faith, your job, your parents, your children, your spouse? Commitment is not to be taken lightly. It comes with a cost. When you commit to something or someone, it becomes almost a sacred oath, if you will, that binds you to something or someone forever.

The commitment of a husband to his wife and of a wife to her husband is sealed with the vows taken in the marriage ceremony. You know, the part that goes "until death do us part." Everything that comes at you both in life will build on that commitment to each other. It goes hand in hand with trust in each other and trust and belief in God, because it is also a commitment to God.

A wife's commitment to her marriage and husband is shown through submission to him first as the head of household (Eph. 5:22–33). The virtues of a good wife are built on the foundation of this commitment. Everything she does is a portrayal of her commitment to her husband. It should mirror all that is good and all that is meant for the good of the marriage and her mate—whether it is raising the children in the admonition of the Lord or going out into the workforce to provide income for family needs.

Husbands, love your wives as you love your own bodies. No one hates his own body, but feeds and cares for it, just as Christ cares for the church.

Chapter 12 Outline

Covetousness in Marriage

    A. Definition
    B. Wants and Needs
    C. God's Law Regarding Covetousness
    D. The Impact on Marriage

References

Exodus 20:17; Colossians 3:5; Hebrews 13:5; Luke 12:15; Mark 6:25; Proverbs 28:2, 21:15, 28:20, 20:21

Discussion

This chapter investigates the negative manifestations of covetousness in marriage. It gives insight into the ramifications of individual needs and wants associated with marriage in our culture. Covetousness, as defined in the law of Moses, will be discussed in relationship to what sets us free or holds us captive as Christians in marriage.

Objectives

Upon review of this chapter, the participants will achieve the following objectives:

1. Discuss the manifestations of covetousness in marriage
2. Define covetousness in a biblical sense
3. List the elements of covetousness that lead to sin in the framework of marriage
4. Recite and discuss the law of Moses that addresses covetousness

Questions

1. Is covetousness ever a positive entity?
2. How can covetousness create discontent in marriage?
3. What sins of covetousness will be revealed, if not resolved, through redemption?
4. How can your way of life be free from the wants of the world while holding on to a healthy marriage?
5. How does the law of Moses determine our freedom or our captivity within the confines of covetousness?
6. What is the difference between covetousness and temptation?
7. How does social media play a role in covetousness?

CHAPTER 12

Covetousness in Marriage

Covetousness is first mentioned in the Bible in Exodus 20:17 KJV as one of the Ten Commandments: "Thou shalt not covet thy neighbor's house, thou shalt not covet thy neighbor's wife, nor his manservant, nor his maidservant, nor his ox, nor his ass, nor anything else that is thy neighbor's." In Deuteronomy 5:21 you will find the Ten Commandments for the covenant community. Moses reemphasizes the Ten Commandments to include "do not covet."

Merriam-Webster's definition of the word *covet* is to want something that you do not have; "to desire what belongs to another inordinately or culpably"; to want, desire, a yearning to have.

Covetousness implies inordinate desire, often for another's possessions. The shackles of covetousness are like quicksand. You sink deeper into a place you prefer not to go. Through the manifestations of covetousness, one can be taken into a deeper and broader sin (1 Cor. 6:9–10). It is set forth as excluding a man from heaven. In a very real sense, it is the root of many other forms of sin (see 1 Tim. 6:9–10; Josh. 7:21; for domestic trouble see Prov. 15:27; Ezek. 22:12).

To desire or want what is not yours makes you, as a person, unhappy with yourself. It makes you unsatisfied with your own personal existence. It pulls you out of your happy zone of contentment and peace and replaces it with a world of turmoil, filled with greed, jealousy, and hate. When out of control, it leads to stealing, lying, and murder. To long for the possessions of others affects the mind, body, and spirit. It attacks your whole sense of well-being. It creates within you spiritual decay that devastates you and your relationship with God. Replace these things with the fruits of the Spirit: love, joy, peace, longsuffering, gentleness, goodness, faith. (Gal. 5:22) KJV

In the context of marriage in the eyes of God, please remember the garden of Eden. Adam and Eve had access to everything in the garden except for the tree of knowledge of good and evil. The devil knows your weaknesses.

Covetousness is a descriptive term for feelings of desire to possess things that belong to someone else—material things in particular. In scripture, covetousness is an egregious act, not at all condoned by God. In marriage, covetousness is often expressed as "keeping up with the Joneses." When one or both spouses start gauging the worth of their marriage by the things other couples have, it can cause great stress in the marriage.

Paul uses the term *greed* to equate with covetousness. In Ephesians 5:3 and 5:5, he states that greed or covetousness is the same as immorality and impurity, so it should be put away. Covetousness becomes the basis for other sins, including theft, murder, and adultery. To commit a covetous sin is to depart from the Ten Commandments. It is a hindrance to godliness and godly service.

Remember that God will supply all of your needs. Just trust Him. Life is truly a struggle, but when you keep God first in the midst of your marriage, He will bless you abundantly—not only with material blessings, but with the spiritual blessings that comes with peace and happiness through the love of God. In millennial terms, let us not be jealous of our neighbors' boats, big-screen TVs, season tickets, and exotic vacations, etc.

How does one get to the point of covetousness in one's marriage? Could it be a personality trait? We have a tendency to be materialistic anyway, and that trait may carry over into marriage. Are we easily influenced by TV ads or showroom floors or visits to friends' houses? Did seeing material goods bring about a "gotta have it" moment?

Scripture warns us not to store up treasures on earth (Matt. 6:19–21). We are to treasure Jesus most of all. Self-centered desires and commitments hinder us from hearing God's Word. They block the blessings and opportunities provided by Jesus to grow and be fruitful.

Do you consider covetousness and temptation to be the same thing? Grammatically, they are different. *Covetousness* is an adjective, while *temptation* is a noun. Covetousness can often lead to temptation, which sparks the action that secures the thing that is desired. This is known as a cause-and-effect reaction that, in most cases, does not bring about good results.

Is covetousness ever good? What if your desire for something motivates you to work more or harder than usual to get what you would like to have? That might seem like a good thing the first or second time you do it, but if this becomes a habit, you can find yourself constantly working overtime, to the extent that you don't spend any time with your spouse or family. It can cause you to lose sight of your original goals or intentions. You might achieve that promotion or make enough money to buy that expensive car, but then you have to take on the added responsibilities of the new position, or pay that exorbitant car note and the expense of upkeep. It kind of digs you into a hole and keeps you there. The more you have, the more you seem to want.

Now this is not to say that we should not want things. Nor does it mean we should not strive to better ourselves. It means simply that we must be sure that all things are in proper perspective according to God's will.

If we think that by fulfilling our covetousness, we will bring about contentment, then we are deceiving ourselves. Contentment comes from doing what we ought to do in the sight of God rather than what we want to do. Service to others in need should be a preference to fulfilling our obsessive desires. "It is more blessed to give than to receive". (Acts 20:35) KJV

How does one deal with covetousness? The first step is to acknowledge it for what it really is. Look for telltale signs. Distinguish it from ordinary wants and desires. Is it affecting the checkbook? Is it interfering with time spent with your spouse and family? Once acknowledged, then go to God in prayer. Confess the sin. Ask for intercession by the Holy Spirit, who will help with the process of repentance and healing.

Covetousness is a channel by which mankind falls from grace, and it happens over time. It corrupts godly character and is shaped by thought patterns and conduct.

What things can you name that could be considered covetous channels or pathways that people pursue? Here are some examples of covetousness in the Bible: Ananias and Sapphira (Acts 5:1–11); Saul (1 Sam. 15:9–19); A-chan (Josh. 7); Judas (Matt. 26:14–15); Balaam (2 Pet. 2:15 with Jude 1:11); David and Bathsheba (2 Sam. 11); and Samson and Delilah (Judg. 16).

Just as in the beginning in Genesis, with Adam and Eve, God has given us freedom within limitations. Marriage is a ceremonial contract with God that has been established with limited freedoms. The law was written by God. The law governs the sense of well-being of couples living in marriages sanctioned by God. Revisit the garden of Eden, where God supplied all the needs of Adam and Eve and asked them not to touch the tree of knowledge of good and evil. But they were tempted by and coveted the fruit of the tree of life.

Compare covetousness with the trunk of a tree that has many branches. These branches are themes we have studied in the Bible, including desire, lust, envy, jealousy, resentment, and hatred.

From desire and lust comes adultery, promiscuity, and sexual immorality that leads to perversion. From envy and jealousy come lying, stealing, bearing false witness, and slanderous behavior. From resentment and hatred come physical harm, murder, and destruction through crimes such as arson. All these things are built upon a slippery slope. We can easily fall into these things. It is a constant struggle in the flesh.

Chapter 13 Outline

Conflict Resolution in Marriage

A. Recognizing Our Differences
B. Reactions to Our Differences
C. Inquire, Don't Confront
D. The Blame Game
E. Anger and the Results of Anger
F. Help from Jesus
G. Forgiveness
H. Methods of Resolution
  1. Yield
  2. Withdraw
  3. Compromise
  4. Resolve
  5. Win

References

Psalms 37:8–9; Proverbs 14:29, 15:1, 16:32; Ephesians 2:14, 4:3, 26, 29, 32; Colossians 3:12, 13; 2 Corinthians 5:19

Discussion

This chapter addresses differences that we as human beings, male and female, bring to marriage. When conflict arises between married couples, their reactions will determine how they handle the situation. Conflict can arise for a number of reasons, including desires, ideas, interests, needs, and goals. The use of anger and its ramifications to resolve conflict will be explored as well as other resolution tactics. The methods by which Jesus resolved conflicts will be noted.

Objectives

Upon review of this chapter, the participants will achieve the following objectives:

1. Describe and explain conflict in marriage
2. Understand the reasons for conflict and the reactions that evolve from conflict
3. Discuss different resolution styles that may be used to work out marital differences
4. Strengthen their marriages through use of appropriate resolution styles when conflict arises
5. Explain how the presence of Jesus Christ in their marriages will help them better resolve conflicts

Questions

1. Name areas of conflict that can occur in marriage.
2. How do you react to conflicts that need resolution?
3. What methods have enhanced the resolution of conflicts in your marriage?
4. How do you deal with anger from your spouse?
5. Has the presence of Jesus Christ in your marriage helped you better resolve your conflicts?
6. Where do empathy and sympathy interact in resolving conflicts in marriage?
7. How can Jesus Christ's teachings be applied to conflict?

CHAPTER 13

Conflict Resolution in Marriage

Resolving conflict is by far the most difficult task to manage. Let us look at how our differences allow us to maneuver through life and deal with different personalities, especially adjusting to the person you married.

Because we are human, we all have our own desires and ideas. Whenever any of these differs from those of our mates, we can find ourselves in conflict. When conflicts arise in marriage—and they will— the manner in which you handle them will set precedent for future conflict resolution.

Resolving differences can be successful when these matters are handled with love patience, maturity, respect, and a few other skills we learn from Galatians 5—the fruits of the Spirit. Practicing the fruits of the Spirit will yield better outcomes. This practice usually wards off a major player in the resolution of conflict: anger. Anger usually occurs when one partner is hurt, threatened, or frustrated by the other. The partner's actions, words, or ways of doing things spark a strong adverse reaction.

The individuality of each partner is based on their gender differences, family life, upbringing, and exposure to the world. We learn how to navigate life as we deal with individuals on all levels, from our parents and siblings to schoolmates and friends to colleagues and competitors in the workplace. In all instances, there have been times of compliance, times of conflict, and times of competition. The way we address these situations will vary. We learn over time, through repetition and exposure, the best way to handle these situations.

Dealing with conflict in marriage requires strength and faith in God and in what He wants for your marriage. The success of your marriage comes from the reason why you married your spouse in the first place. The reason has to be greater than the stress you are under at any given time.

When we marry, we become one in God's Word and in God's will. We should be in submission to God's will, and we should submit to each other in the fear of God. Ephesians 2:14 KJV says, "For He is our peace, who hath made both one and hath broken down the middle wall of partition between us." KJV Ephesians 4:3 says, "Endeavoring to keep the unity of the Spirit in the bind if peace." KJV This in itself will keep Christ in the center of your marriage.

When we find ourselves in conflict in marriage, regardless of the reason, it is our reaction to the differences causing the stress between us that determines the outcome and the strength of the marriage going forward. Studies in conflict resolution offer strategies that can be used to resolve differences between conflicting partners. Many of these strategies warn against allowing emotions to overrule our judgment. Anger, fear, distrust, and betrayal are some of the emotions that can result in blaming, confronting, speaking, and doing irrational things that may cause regret later on. Methods of resolution include compromise, withdrawal, yielding, and winning by any means necessary under the will of God. All methods considered, the most Christlike actions include listening, communicating truthfully, being respectful to each other, apologizing when in the wrong, asking for forgiveness, praying, and forgiving.

Conflict resolution should always be taken to God in prayer for repentance, guidance, direction, and forgiveness. Both partners should remember their marriage commitment to each other. In the Bible, 2 Corinthians 5:18–19 speaks of reconciliation. When Jesus is present in the marriage, reconciliation can be made with a deeper understanding of the differences between you and a deeper love for your partner.

Chapter 14 Outline

Financial Assets and Liabilities in Marriage

A. Financial Goals
    1. Assets and Liabilities
    2. God, Finances, and Marriage
    3. Temptation and Debt
    4. Short-Range and Long-Range Financial Goals
B. Economic Theories
    1. Budget
    2. Credit Cards
    3. Planning for the Unexpected
    4. Investment
    5. Savings
    6. Tithing

References

Genesis 2:24; Proverbs 10:22; Psalms 24:1; Deuteronomy 8:18; Proverbs 22:1; 1 Timothy 6:6–10; Luke 6:28; Romans 13:8–10; Ecclesiastes 5:19; Malachi 3:10

Discussion

Management of financial assets and liabilities can place a strain upon the marital relationship. This chapter explores the financial peaks and valleys of marriage. There will be highs and lows as bills come and go. Sharing money will be discussed, along with the many facets of cost as it relates to rent, food, transportation, taxes, and so on. Many costs are unforeseen. It is a known fact that the foundation of financial unity in marriage is a mutual commitment to a biblical philosophy of money management.

Objectives

Upon review of this chapter, the participants will achieve the following objectives:

1. Have a more insightful approach to finances in marriage
2. Investigate current economic theories that are being used as cutthroat economics
3. Have a higher awareness of predatory lending practices
4. List four undesirable instruments for debt in marriage
5. Cover pitfalls that create strain on finances in marriage
6. Prioritize budgeting their spending to meet their needs as the marriage progresses
7. Tithe

Questions

1. How may married couples resolve financial situations that place a strain on the marriage?
2. What are some of the warning signals that lead to bad debt?
3. How can poor financial choices be limited in a given marriage?
4. What role does God play in your marriage finances?
5. How do stewardship and discipleship work in marriage and the church?

CHAPTER 14

Financial Assets and Liabilities in Marriage

One of the greatest obstacles that come with marriage is the financial baggage that both partners bring into the marriage. Assets may include an automobile or automobiles that are paid off, furniture and other material goods that have been paid for, good credit ratings, employment, retirement plans, and educational qualifications. Liabilities include automobiles with unpaid loans, other loans with high interest rates, low credit scores, student loans, tuition bills, taxes owed, and unforeseen costs such as loss of income (unemployment) and medical bills.

We suggest that assets and liabilities be merged and that incomes be merged into one bank account. This creates an interdependence and interrelationship for the couple to bond over. It creates a communication bond regarding payment of bills and the purchase of food, clothing, and entertainment. Married couples need to factor in safe, affordable housing and insurance.

In Genesis, when God gave control of the earth to man, He ordered Adam to take possession to till, to subdue, and to have dominion. The two humans were combined as one. So shall their salaries, assets, and liabilities be united into one. The spouses will begin to unite in shared responsibilities. We suggest that the couple get together and list all their assets and liabilities separately. From that point, they can create a plan to remove the liabilities. This can be done by prioritizing what will work in a budget and what will not work (Gen. 2:24; Eph. 5:31).

Regardless of the assets and liabilities you bring to the marriage, remember that "the blessing of the Lord it maketh rich and He addeth no sorrow with it". (Prov. 10:22) KJV. So, continue to believe and trust in God, and He will work in your married lives to help you overcome your financial obstacles.

Be leery of obsession with riches, because wealth opens doors to other possibilities that are in defiance of the Lord's will. The love of money is the root of all kinds of evil. Some people, craving money, have wandered from the true faith and harmed themselves in many ways (1 Tim. 6:10). This does not mean that God doesn't want you to have things or to have a good life, but be cautious of how you use the riches God provides for you. Keep Jesus in your life. When God blesses you with riches, He will give you good health to enjoy it.

Married couples must base their finances around taxes. These are some factors that may be considered:

- Be aware of income taxes before and in marriage.
- Beware of spikes in income based on jobs obtained after college, promotions, new jobs, and raises.
- Beware of jumping to buy a brand-new house or brand-new cars too soon. Although you may be able to afford them according to your income, be mindful of the taxes that accompany increases in salary, and the other financial liabilities that will be incurred. Not only are you buying the house or car, but the cost of utilities, insurance, gasoline, and other operating costs must be taken into consideration.
- Debt is a fluid element that can be good one day and bad the next day.
- Newlyweds and married couples need to be aware of fluctuating credit scores. Scores can change after the loss of employment, job transfers, and relocations.

- Be leery of credit card solicitations and credit lenders whose objectives are to make money and leave you in a world of despair.
- Be wary of preapproved credit or offers of credit cards. They reduce your credit score with each inquiry while offering ridiculously high interest rates.
- Beware of spending beyond your budget, such as on special occasions and holidays like Christmas and Easter.

In Keith Carter's (2009) book, *Yes, I Can Set My House in Order*, he says there are four purposes for a budget:

- to get out of debt
- to plan in advance
- to know where your money is going
- to maximize the power of your money

Carter creates guidelines and indicators of monthly cash flow, highlights where your greatest debt is, and highlights needs when setting priorities. Your budget and debt flow are not consistent throughout your life and marriage. As indebtedness increases, the budget has to be adjusted in order to keep it in balance.

Be leery of the trap of "robbing Peter to pay Paul." Although there will be times when it is necessary to do so, please keep in mind that Peter must be repaid. This applies especially in unforeseen or unexpected occurrences, which will happen. Pay your bills on time.

Planning in advance allows you to budget for trips, vacations, and reunions without taking out loans to cover expenses.

It is important to know where your money is going. Establish short-range and long-range financial goals. It helps to plan for the education of your children, for retirement, and possibly for extended care needs.

How and where you invest your money is key to financial planning. Whether you invest in a home, 401(k)s, stocks and bonds, or money markets, always consider the retirement plans offered where you work. Check your status regarding social security. If it is possible for you to pay into it, it will benefit you in retirement. This is another way of investing in your future.

If you have children, it's advisable to teach them at an early age about the value and the use of a good money plan. Learning to save in childhood and becoming knowledgeable about money early in life are important. The earlier children learn how to manage money, the better equipped they will be to make intelligent money decisions in adulthood.

Managing the power of your money is a long-range consideration and takes years to develop. During your early years of marriage, you may not be able to see the payoff, but on the other side of midlife, it will bring you great reward. Long-range and short-range goals should always be emphasized in family growth and marriage.

Keep God in your life. If possible, tithe. If it is difficult to do so, God knows your heart. Give what you can through discipleship and stewardship.

Prenuptial agreements might be considered when married partners bring inherited wealth or personal business wealth to the union, which may require legal assessment.

Regardless of your circumstances as you enter the marriage arena, God will provide for you. God knows your heart, your desires, and your ambitions. Pray. Pray together, and God will see you through. He has His own plans for your marriage.

Chapter 15 Outline

The Impact of Social Media on Marriage

    A. Social Media Defined
    B. Original Intent
    C. Common Use
    D. Useful versus Harmful
    E. Trust Factors
    F. God's Intent
    G. Marital Impact
    H. Other Modes of Social Media

References

Luke 11:34; Philippians 4:8; Psalm 101:3–4; 1 Thessalonians 5:21–22; 1 Corinthians 15:33; Matthew 6:22–23; 1 John 2:15–17; 1 Corinthians 6:12–13

Discussion

There is an increasing trend toward using social media tools for many kinds of services, including professional relationships, interpersonal relationships, and political networking. This chapter will look at the impact social media has had on marriages and the various means of managing social media in marriage.

Objectives

Upon review of this chapter, the participants will achieve the following objectives:

1. Understand the various social media tools
2. Realize the effects social media has on history and memory

3. Discuss the impact of social media on marriage (e.g., time use, privacy, ownership of content, interpersonal relationships)

Questions

1. In your opinion, how is social media affecting marriages today?
2. In your opinion, how is social media affecting your life personally, as far as history and memory are concerned? Is it good or bad?
3. How much time is spent using media in your home?
4. What harm can you see social media doing to your home?

CHAPTER 15
The Impact of Social Media on Marriage

With current advancements in technology and the unparalleled popularity of it, the inevitable acceptance of social media in our daily married lives has become pervasive and, in many ways, necessary. Computer- and phone-based social media allow the creation of forms of expression that can be shared within communities, between individuals, and on networks. Web-based applications such as texting, commenting, and posting of videos, photos, and data generated by the user are some of the most commonly used features of social media. Social media also includes service-specific profiles that are designed and maintained by the user, connecting them to other individuals or groups. This explanation of the features of social media defines the original intent for the use of these technological services.

Tablets, smartphones, and other mobile devices use web-based technology as a means of interaction whereby individuals, businesses, and organizations conduct business, moving away from traditional modes of communication such as newspapers, television, and radio. Web-based technology is appealing because of the immediate accessibility of information and the ease and breadth of its use.

Individuals, corporations, entrepreneurs, nonprofit organizations and even governments have experienced both negative and positive impacts of social media. A personal sense of connectedness and effective marketing are benefits on the positive side. Negatively, however, the excessive use of social media has been associated with "cyberbullying" or harassment.

How is social media affecting marriage? How is it most commonly used in marriages? Is it useful or harmful to marriage? Let us look at the impact of social media on marriage.

Social media may maintain a strong bond of communication between partners when they are apart, such as when one partner is out of town on a business trip or away because of the illness of a relative. Even when married couples are at home, the new technology helps them communicate effectively to coordinate errands, picking up the children from school, and the like.

There are many modes of communication couples enjoy currently. Couples must be up-front and let each other know which applications they are connected to. It is important to note that information about your personal lives will be out there for all to see. Résumés and vitae are often placed on social media networks such as LinkedIn if the couple is upwardly mobile and seeking to advance in their professional careers. Social media is also a good way to keep up with classmates who have the same aspirations. Things may be worked out more smoothly when both parties know the media being used.

Facebook is a social network that innocently shares information and photos with friends who are linked. There is a note of caution to sound when a spouse places themselves out there and not with their partner. Although you are married, and that fact is established in your profile, nevertheless you have put pictures of yourself out there. As innocent as this may be in your heart, the demons are always around, seeking to devour and destroy whomever they can find.

The smartphone has transformed our society with a new dimension of communication. The common cell phone has morphed into a miraculous personal electronic life form that keeps you connected all day and all night. A smartphone has applications that enable you to receive any kind of information within seconds of your inquiry.

Applications that are designed for social interaction may be fun to use between married couples, family, and friends. As married couples engage in the social media, from a godly point of view, please keep all avenues in the realm of Christian living. Your friends on social media need to be like-minded believers in Christ. Your business and professional relations on social media must be centered around wholesome Christian living.

As you protect your home environment, centered in Christ, please consider protecting your social media environment in the same way. Allow the Spirit of the Lord to manifest through your texts and email messages. Bible verses and prayers are devices that elevate strength and trust, keeping a marriage strong while uplifting the people around you. The Covid-19 pandemic has increased the use of Zoom, Facebook and YouTube, helping Christians to stay connected to their churches and Christian brothers and sisters. We connect via Zoom to church services, Sunday school, and Bible study. God will find a way to keep His Word alive.

Chapter 16 Outline

Health and Wellness

    A. Letting Yourself Go
    B. Sickness: General
    C. Sickness: Specific
    D. Injury and Accidents
    E. Personal Hygiene
    F. Physical Fitness
    G. Healthy Eating

References

Proverbs 3:7-8, 4:20–22, 1 Corinthians 3:16-17; Romans 12:1-2; Psalm 103:2–3

Discussion

The maintenance of good health and hygiene is important in marriage. It affects aspects of the marital covenant ranging from intimacy and respect to devotion and honoring your vows. This chapter will explore the effects that hygiene and illness have on the married couple and their covenanted responsibilities.

Objectives

Upon review of this chapter, the participants will achieve the following objectives:

1. Understand the role of a spouse in the event of illness

2. Determine the effect one's illness will have on the marriage
3. Be able to honestly and factually discuss sexually transmitted diseases with each other and with your children when it is necessary
4. Listen to and understand, from the medical experts, the total ramifications of your spouse's injury or illness
   a. short-term recovery
   b. long-term recovery
5. Discuss the role of prayer in sickness and injuries
6. Discuss expectations of hygiene with their spouse and teens
7. Be prepared for the unexpected

Questions

1. What do you do when your spouse exhibits poor hygiene habits?
2. What do you do when your spouse becomes ill?
3. How significant is prayer to illness and recovery?
4. Do you pray for the health and well-being of your spouse? Your other family members?
5. Do you reflect on your wedding vows, which include "in sickness and in health" and "till death do us part"?
6. How do you prepare for the unexpected?

CHAPTER 16

Health and Wellness

The significance of marriage to good health is proven by medical research. Married people tend to live longer, perhaps due to the fact that they have someone to live with and live for. When you have a dedicated Christian married partner, it means you will be together for life— "as long as ye both shall live"—and through all circumstances— "for richer, for poorer, in sickness and in health." These factors can give mental security, stability, and peace of mind when trust is established and a covenant is shared before God. When the trials of life come along, the assurance of a partner who will endure with you reduces the stress and worry that you experience.

Married couples tend to look out for each other. They encourage each other to eat healthier, exercise more, and engage in social activities together. They make plans to do things they enjoy together, giving them hope and an expectation of having a future together. They also tend to discourage unhealthy habits and risky endeavors, thereby reducing patterns of self-destruction. Symptoms are detected early. Couples support each other during illness and recovery, which can boost the immune system and reduce the probability of getting sick in the first place.

Marriage seems to have a kind of protective influence over migraine headaches, viruses like the flu, and even more serious health conditions like cancer and heart disease. This is not to say that marriage can prevent these things from happening, but it appears to lessen the frequency or the seriousness of the condition.

When children are part of the marriage, these traits of support, nurturing, and encouragement carry over to the children, causing them to be healthier, happier, and more stable as they grow and develop.

As we look at health and wellness in marriage, there are some intimate details that require attention. As stated in 1 Peter, the human body is God's holy temple, formed in the likeness of God. "Be not wise in thine own eyes: fear the Lord and depart from evil. It shall be health to thy navel, and marrow to thy bones." (Proverbs 3:7–8) KJV. Tradition religious teachers use these scripture passages as a symbolic representation of what it means to be blessed with good physical health.

When we get married, we must at all times respect each other's privacy. Things like getting dressed and bathing come to mind.

Personal hygiene is most significant when you are young in your marriage and when you begin to grow older in your marriage. If you married in your twenties, on the basis of age alone, the majority of couples should experience a healthy lifestyle. Taking time to work out and go out on the town on a regular basis after work are in line with a healthy lifestyle. It is suggested that healthy exercises like playing tennis on a regular basis, followed by taking a few laps around the old track is good to energize your health in marriage. This type of exercise creates a strong, healthy body, mentally and physically.

During this time in your marriage, you may agree to have a baby. There is no great formula or secret. A healthy body may produce healthy children.

Most people assume that the younger they are, the fewer health problems they should experience. Consider the lifestyle of your intended spouse. Did you meet in church? In college? On the job? Or did you meet at a party or a night club? How many people have you been familiar with? We are making it real because health and science are real.

There are many infectious diseases circulating in the public sphere that may be checked for before marriage. Such diseases may have genetic implications in starting a family. These infections include HIV, HPV, syphilis, gonorrhea, trichomonas, candida/yeast, and chlamydia, to name a few. All are associated with urogenital diseases or infections.

In years past, a blood test was required by most state health departments as part of the process of getting a marriage license. The blood test was documented to ensure that both partners would have a healthy start and healthy babies.

If one of these infections shows up in your partner, please get treatment for both of you, so you do not pass the infection to each other over and over. Such diseases, if they become chronic, may affect a newborn baby, or your internal organs later on. This information comes from the authors who are legitimate health care professionals and we are very familiar with the manifestations and consequences of these conditions.

As we age, our bodies will take on acute and noticeable changes. Suits and dress sizes will increase right before our eyes, with or without children, though change will be more apparent for those who have children. Along with acute weight gain in middle age, medical conditions may arise. Please be aware of metabolic syndrome, obesity, high blood pressure, and diabetes. We caution you to be cognizant of your health as you both mature in your marriage.

Blood pressure is the leading condition that results in some form of heart disease. Annual checkups are highly recommended to monitor your health. Some problems may have hidden factors that can be detected early, so that you and your physician will be on course to prevent sickness. Blood pressure checks are easily done, sometimes even at the pharmacy. Use common sense. Lowering sodium or salt intake and increasing hydration will go a very long way. Be aware of the effect cough medicines and tablets can have on blood pressure. Please make sure the ones you take over the counter are approved by your doctor and do not elevate your blood pressure. This is especially important if you are suffering from allergies and sinus conditions. Try to keep stress at a lower level. Keep exercising, dancing, and laughing. Remember to watch how much and what you eat.

Obesity is a precursor to metabolic syndrome. Weight control is the most difficult health problem to manage while all systems of the human body are stable. Please maintain a normal body mass index (BMI) based on your age and your height. Maintaining a perfect weight is a lifelong pursuit.

Type 2 diabetes is the manifestation of all things gone wrong. In most patients, it results from excessive food intake and the wrong kind of food—high in calories, high in sugar, and high in cholesterol, which overwhelms insulin production in the pancreas. If you add to this excessive drinking of alcohol, it overwhelms the endocrine system.

When the doctor tells you that you are borderline diabetic, blow the whistle at that very moment and *stop*! Change your lifestyle immediately. Cut your cholesterol level in half. Take precautionary steps to safely lose weight and improve your wellness for your spouse, yourself, and your children.

Most people have to wait until they are diagnosed as diabetic before their doctors refer them to a health information class. Such a class gives you a great deal of information about prevention and things to avoid. Waiting until diagnosis to refer patients to the class is like shutting the barn door after the horse is out. As part of your annual exam, ask your physician to refer you to a diabetes class if he or she believes it could benefit you now, even if you haven't been formally diagnosed.

Health and wellness are definitely works in progress as we live each day, glorifying God along the way. Seniors in marriage find themselves living on the edge of the unexpected each day. Not to discourage you, but this time is when trust in the Living God is supreme (Ps. 122). My God watches over us day and night, and we rest in His sheltering arms.

Each spouse should know and understand their partner's medical conditions and daily medications. We suggest keeping a list of your partner's prescriptions and vitamins in your wallet or purse at all times, in case of an emergency.

Know that you both are devoted partners, looking after each other's every need. When surgeries occur, be there every morning and evening in the hospital. Never leave your spouse's side. Yes, this is old-fashioned, just like the old-fashioned religion expressed in the marital covenant. Assist your spouse home from the hospital and help in their at-home care while they become well again. Such direction is added to God's blessings on you and your family.

APPENDIX

An Exercise in Communication

1. Describe different ways communication can break down in a marriage.

2. List nonverbal traits that you observe in your spouse's behavior that leads to a breakdown in communication.

3. Note personality traits that lead to communication breakdown in a marriage.

4. Describe modes of verbal and nonverbal communication that may have a positive or negative impact on marriage.

Positive Impact   Negative Impact

1. Describe different ways communication can break down in a marriage.
   - stress
   - nuances due to personal or spiritual maturity or immaturity
   - double standards

2. List nonverbal traits that you observe in your spouse's behavior that leads to a breakdown in communication.
   - low tone of voice
   - short answers, limited conversation
   - won't eat
   - rubbernecking
   - body stance
   - gestures
   - rolling the eyes

3. Note personality traits that lead to communication breakdown in a marriage.
   - indecisive
   - inclined to worry
   - internalizes feelings

4. Describe modes of verbal and nonverbal communication that may have a positive or negative impact on marriage.

Positive Impact	Negative Impact
Sometimes not communicating allows for time to think things through.	Not saying you need time to think will hurt the relationship.
You have to allow your spouse time to think things through.	Not allowing your spouse time to think can have a negative impact.

104

REFERENCES

Carter, Keith K. (2009) *"Yes, I Can, Set My House In Order"*. Oklahoma City, The Love Group.

Wright, Norm H. & Roberts and Wes Roberts. 1997. *Before You Say I Do: A Marriage Preparation Manual for Couples*. Accessed, 2016. Eugene, Oregon. Harvest House Publishers.

The Holy Bible. King James Version

Additional Resources

Andrews, Otis and Deigie. 1994. *Husbands and Wives*. Nashville: Lifeway Press.

Cohen, Sheldon, William Doyle, David P. Skoner, Bruce S. Rabin, and Jack Gwaltney Jr. 1997. "Social Ties and Susceptivity to the Common Cold." *Journal of the American Medical Association* 277 (1997): 1940–44.

Crandfield, Ken R. 1992. *Seven Secrets of Effective Fatherhood*. Wheaton, IL: Tyndale House.

Dungy, Tony, and Lauren Dungy. 2014. *Uncommon Marriage*. Carol Stream, IL: Tyndale House of Publishers.

Eggerichs, Emerson. 2004. *Love and Respect*. Cengage Learning Center, Boston, Massachusetts.

Herbert, Miles J. 1967. *Sexual Happiness in Marriage*. Grand Rapids, MI: Zondervan.

Hu, Yuaureng, and Noreen Goldman. 1990. "Mortality Differentials by Marital Status: An International Comparison." *Demography* 27: 233–50.

Kiecolt-Glaser, Janice K., and Tamara L. Newton. 2001. "Marriage and Health; His and Hers." *Psychological Bulletin* 127: 472–503.

Lewis, Robert. 2003. *The Quest for Authentic Manhood*. Nashville: Lifeway Press.

Mack, Wayne A. 1999. *Strengthening Your Marriage*. Phillipsburg, NJ: P&R Publishing.

Matthews, D. Wayne. "Marriage Enrichment: Communication in Marriage." *Family and Consumer Sciences.*Raleigh, North Carolina Cooperative Extension Service.

Omartian, Stormie. 1997. *The Power of a Praying Wife*. Eugene, OR: Honest House Publishers.

Rice, Shirley. 1967. *The Christian Home*. Norfolk, VA: Norfolk Christian Schools.

Sproul, R. C. 1975. *Discovering the Intimacies of Marriage*. Minneapolis: Bethany Fellowship.

Swiggum, Harley. 2011. *The Bethel Series*. Madison, WI: The Adult Christian Education Foundation.

Taylor, Robert Jr. 1973. *Christ in the Home*. Grand Rapids, MI: Baker.

Wright, Norman. *Developing Spiritual Intimacy in Marriage*. Accessed 2016. http://www.familylife.com/articles/topics/marriage/staying-married/growing-spiritually/developing-spiritual-intimacy-in-marriage

As an overall gesture, married couples should never take each other, or any aspect of their family relationships for granted. Every topic discused in this book is important to the success of your marriage and is not to be taken lightly. Marriages that last for five or more decades have endured many disappointments, trials, celebrations and the unforeseen. Marriages that have kept God at its center, or first, tend to overcome the trials and rejoice even in the midst of unforeseen occurrences and disappointments. Their successes can also be attributed to the ability of the marriage partners to show patience to one another, as well as respect and forgiveness as they realize neither partner is perfect, but each partner deserves his or her honesty and trust.

As this discussion of marriage comes to an end, we would like to impress upon the reader(s) a few common themes which reappear throughout the book. First, the theme of reflection is to always put God first in everything you do as a married couple. Second, if things you ask for are in His will, they will be answered according to His time and purpose. Third, as you progress in your marriage from year to year, keep the Lord constantly present through daily prayer, and if time permits, meditation.

Don't ever forget that there is no perfect marriage. It will always be a work in progress. When you mess up or make a crucial mistake, always ask for forgiveness from your mate and be constantly ready for reconciliation. Repent and ask for forgiveness from the Lord, then ask for forgiveness from your spouse, and remember how many times Jesus tells us to forgive, 70 times 7, Matthew 18:22, and in your marriage that should be easily achieved.

ACKNOWLEDGMENTS

With great appreciation, we would like to acknowledge our parents, Mr. James "Butch" and Ernestine Hamilton and Mr. John A. and Ruth Townsend. Our parents made a wonderful example to us as children growing up in Christian homes. The manifestation of their faith in God through prayer and worship enabled us to have a heritage we have been able to follow throughout life.

Special Recognition

We would like to recognize the St. John Missionary Baptist Church, Oklahoma City, Oklahoma, specifically under the direction of Rev. Dr. Major Jemison, pastor, and Rev. Dr. Lawrence Kirk, director of Christian education, who approached us about developing a married couples' Enrichment Hour during Sunday School Enrichment Hour. They provided the space and resources for us to compile this work, which the Lord has brought to full fruition. For this we are deeply appreciative.

Printed in the United States
by Baker & Taylor Publisher Services

Printed in the United States
by Baker & Taylor Publisher Services